Skill Development in INDIA

Skill Development in INDIA

Dr. B. Ramaswamy
Dr. R. Sasikala Pushpa
Dr. M.B. Gururaj

PRABHAT
PAPERBACKS

Publisher

PRABHAT PAPERBACKS

4/19 Asaf Ali Road, New Delhi–110 002

Ph. 23289555 • 23289666 • 23289777 • Helpline/ 7827007777

e-mail: prabhatbooks@gmail.com • Website: www.prabhatbooks.com

Price

Four Hundred Rupees

ISBN 978-93-5322-280-2

Printed at

SS Japan Arts, Delhi

SKILL DEVELOPMENT IN INDIA

by Dr. B. Ramaswamy, Dr. R. Sasikala Pushpa & Dr. M.B. Gururaj

Published by **PRABHAT PAPERBACKS**

4/19 Asaf Ali Road, New Delhi–110 002

ISBN 978-93-5322-280-2

₹ 400.00

About the Authors

DR. B. RAMASWAMY'S BRIEF BIO-DATA

Dr. B. Ramaswamy is a Social Scientist, Educator, Author & Motivator. He was the Pro-Vice Chancellor of Oriental University, Indore, Madhya Pradesh & APG Shimla University, Shimla, Himachal Pradesh.

Currently he is working as a Professor and Chair (National Education Foundation) for Skill Development in the State University of New York, USA which is the largest university of USA.

Member- Advisory Committee- For the National Commission for Protection of Child Rights (NCPCR), Govt. of India

Member- Divisional Railway Users' Consultative Committee (DRUCC) on Railways of Chennai Division, Govt. of India

Member to the Centre of IT and Social Science, Indraprastha Institute of Information Technology (IIIT), Govt. of Delhi

Member- Doctoral Advisory Committee, Indraprastha Institute of Information Technology (IIIT), Govt. of Delhi

He has obtained all his qualifications from reputed institutions and universities such as Loyola College, Delhi School of Economics, National Law University etc. Apart from his exemplary achievements in the field of Sociology, academically and professionally, he has several other qualifications and professional achievements in the fields of Disaster Management, Journalism and Mass Communication, Human Rights, IPR, Cyber Law, Personnel Management and Industrial Relations, Vedic Culture, Leadership, Issues of Women and Children, Disability Studies etc. He has done Honorary Doctorate from Cosmopolitan University (USA), & Inter- American University of Humanistic Studies, Florida (USA), in the field of Social Science. He was also awarded Honorary Doctorate on Humanities in Apostolic International University, affiliated with and accredited by International Institute of Church Management Inc., Florida, USA. Recently he was awarded D.Litt (Development Economics) from International EconomicsUniversity, Maldives. He has guided M. Phil. and Ph. D. scholars on his competent areas. He is a Visiting Fellow, Advisor, Member in several prestigious Institutions both in Government and Private such as IIT Roorkee, YASHADA, Raj Bhawan, Pune and NIPCCD, Govt. of India, Delhi. He has published more than 250 articles/ books both in National and International magazines/ publication of repute.

He continues to write articles to leading magazines and newspapers. Being a renowned Social Scientist, he is invited as Speaker to deliver key note addresses and as a Chief Guest to various functions, seminars, national and international conferences, Convocations and workshops. He has travelled to more than 19 countries to deliver lectures in various areas. He motivates large number of youth including the school children. He makes tremendous impact while delivering each lecture which brings tremendous mind transformation in the youth of India. He holds important positions in Government viz Member, Maintenance Tribunal- Maintenance and Welfare of Parents and Senior Citizen Act 2007. He also worked as Deputy Chief Warden- Civil Defence Corps, Delhi and as Director in many Institutions and Private bodies. He was an acting Chairperson, Child Welfare Committee, Government of NCT, Delhi – A bench of Magistrates constituted under section 29 of Juvenile Justice. Being an expert Social Scientist and Educationist, he is interviewed regularly by the various electronic media, TV channels and Press. His passion is directed towards our nation building through quality education especially to those who are deprived of quality education. He has so far produced more than 1000 civil service officers in the country.

BRIEF BIO DATA

Dr. Sasikala Pushpa has been the Member of Parliament (RajyaSabha). She completed her B.A. (English Literature) from University of Madras, Chennai and M.A. (Public Administration) from University of Madras, Chennai. She has also done Diploma in Business Administration from the Southern Cross University, Singapore. Her Ph.D. in Public Administration is from Manonmaniyam Sundaranar University, Tamil Nadu.

She has been an ardent political and social worker, teacher and educationist. Earlier, she served as the Mayor of Thoothukudi Corporation, Tamil Nadu. She also held positions like: Member, Parliament Committee on Human Resource Development (MHRD); Member, Parliament Committee of Privileges; and Member, Parliament Committee of Women and Children at national level.

She is a proficient Bharatanatyam dancer. She enjoys coaching IAS aspirants. In this direction, she has been organizing free IAS Training Centers in rural Tamil Nadu for the Below Poverty Line (BPL) youths. She has been running a full-fledged IAS academy for the last 14 years which produced more than 1000 civil services officers for the country. She has provided career guidance to students in various colleges across Tamil Nadu; and has organized developmental activities for rural women to impart training, skills and to engage them in income generation activities. She has held positions like: Joint Secretary (Women Wing, A.I.A.D.M.K., 2009); Deputy Secretary (Youth Brigade Wing, A.I.A.D.M.K., 2010); and Secretary (Women Wing, A.I.A.D.M.K., 2013). She has been associated with development of sports in rural areas of Tamil Nadu.

Countries visited by her include, South Korea (as a member of the delegation sponsored by the Government of South Korea for World Mayors Conference on Climate Change in 2013); South Africa (as a member of the delegation sponsored by the Government of South Africa for World Youth Conference in 2010); and Singapore. She has been selected to go as a parliament delegate for deliberation on the 137th assembly of Inter – Parliamentary Union in St. Petersburg, Russian Federation in 2017. Recently she had gone for education visit to various universities in Belgium, London, Netherland, France,State University of New York, USA etc. (2018). She specializes in research on British Administration. She is a prolific writer and commentator. She has authored more than 4 books and written more than 20 articles in leading journals and magazines.

PROF (DR) M.B. GURURAJ'S BRIEF BIO-DATA

Prof (Dr) M.B. Gururaj is a well-known Human Resource Specialist, Educator, Unique Trainer in STEM & Employability Education. Earlier he was Head of the various organizations & institutions in public and private sectors in India and abroad. He has attained experience and exposure in the areas of Business Development, HR, Training and Organizational Development.

Currently, Prof (Dr) MB Gururaj

President- National Education Foundation (NEF) USA & State University of New York

President- National Education Foundation India (NEF) & Global

Advisor- National Skill Development Corporation (NSDC) India

Chief Mentor Izen, Technology Company USA

President- National Education Foundation (NEF) Stem Global Academy India and US

He has obtained his Degree and Post Qualification from reputed institutions in India and research in Industrial Psychology. He has exemplary success in Human Resource Development, setting up of Organizations, International Relations and Training Specialist.

He has been a Great Communicator, Public Speaker and successfully handled business and execution of projects.

He has served for more than two decades in public sector and government at various levels in HR, Contracts and International Business. Subsequent to gaining experience in Public Sector, he held the positions of Head of HR and Chairman of universities and got involved in Unique Industry Academia Relations, trained more than 8 lac students in Engineering, Management and served various State Governments and NSDC in their endeavour of skilling of youth for better tomorrow and making them industry ready.

He has been a Motivator in Relationship Management and Brand Building. He has also authored various Modules in training of Youth, Women and Entrepreneurship.

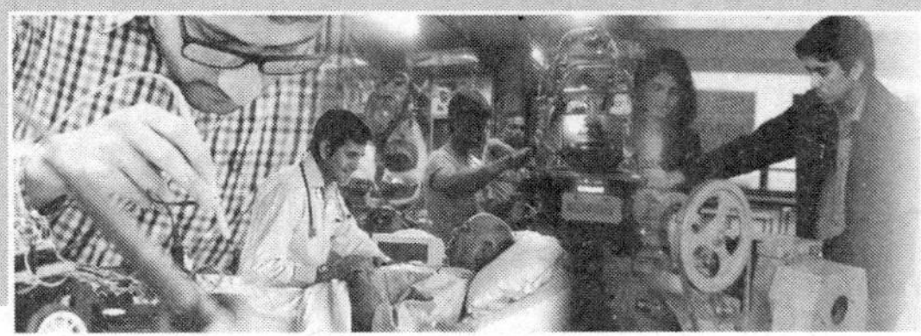

Acronyms

• AA	Assessment Agency
• AAP	Annual Action Plan
• AICTE	All India Council for Technical Education
• ASDP	Aajeevika Skill Development Programme
• ASSOCHAM	Associated Chambers of Commerce and Industry of India
• ATS	Advanced Training Scheme
• BDO	Block Development Officer
• CBSE	Central Board of Secondary Education
• CHSE	Council of Higher Secondary Education
• CIDC	Construction Industry Development Council
• CII	Confederation of Indian Industries
• CJM	Chief Judicial Magistrate
• CTC	Cost to Company
• CTS	Craftsmen Training Scheme
• DGET	Directorate General of Employment and Training
• DLO	District Labour Officer
• DM	District Magistrate
• DoPT	Department of Personnel and Training
• FICCI	Federation of Indian Chambers of Commerce and Industry

- GDP Gross Domestic Product
- GoI Government of India
- GP Gram Panchayat
- ILO International Labour Organization
- ISTD Indian Society for Training & Development
- ITI Industrial Training Institute
- J&K Jammu and Kashmir
- MLA Member of Legislative Assembly
- MES-SDI Modular Employability Scheme-Skill Development Initiative
- MHRD Ministry of Human Resource Development
- MHUPA Ministry of Housing and Urban Poverty Alleviation
- MoLE Ministry of Labour and Employment
- MoRD Ministry of Rural Development
- MP Member of Parliament
- MSDE Ministry of Skill Development and Entrepreneurship
- MSME Ministry of Micro, Small and Medium Enterprises
- NABET National Accreditation Board for Education and Training
- NBSC National Board for Skill Certification
- NCVT National Council of Vocational Training
- N-E North-East
- NIOS National Institute of Open Schooling
- NOS National Occupational Standards
- NPMC National Project Management Cell
- NSDA National Skill Development Agency
- NSDC National Skill Development Corporation
- NSQC National Skills Qualifications Committee
- NSQF National Skills Qualifications Framework
- NULM National Urban Livelihoods Mission

- NVEQF — National Vocational Education Qualification Framework
- NVQF — National Vocational Qualification Framework
- PAN — Permanent Account Number
- PIA — Project Implementing Agency
- PMC — PMKVY Monitoring Committee
- PMKVY — Pradhan Mantri Kaushal Vikas Yojana
- PMU — Project Management Unit
- PwD — Persons with Disability
- QCI — Quality Council of India
- QP — Qualification Packs
- RDAT — Regional Directorates of Apprenticeship Training
- RPL — Recognition of Prior Learning
- SAR — Self-Assessment Report/Self-Audit Report
- SCVT — State Council for Vocational Training
- SDI — Skills Development Initiative
- SDM — Sub Divisional Magistrate
- SDMS — Skill Development Management System
- SGSY — Swarnajayanti Gram Swarozgar Yojana
- SKP — Skill Knowledge Providers
- SOP — Standard Operating Procedure
- SRLM — State Rural Livelihood Mission
- SSC — Sector Skills Council
- STAR — Standard Training Assessment and Rewards
- STEP — Support to Training and Employment Program (under the portfolio of MHRD)
- TAFE — Technical and Further Education (Australia)
- TC — Training Centre
- TFP — Total Factor Productivity
- ToT — Training of Trainer
- TP — Training Partner

- TRYSEM — Training of Youth for Self-Employment (GOI program)
- UGC — University Grants Commission (within the MHRD portfolio)
- UT — Union Territory
- VET — Vocational Education and Training

❑❑❑

Contents

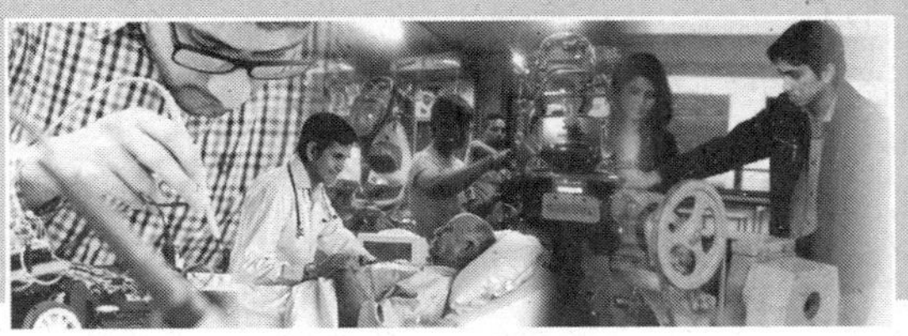

Chapter 1

Education and Skill Development for 21st Century

The benefits of a growing economy are often reflected in the growing number of well-paid jobs in a country. Consequently, any policy that stimulates the economy to grow, has an impact on job creation and the overall employability of the country's workforce. India finds itself in a context today where young people are entering the workforce every year. To make the most of the demographic dividend, it is critical to improve the employability of the youth. For this, the newly set up Ministry of Skill Development and Entrepreneurship had taken up the task of coordinating all skill development efforts across the country. This includes the removal of the disconnect between demand and supply of skilled manpower, building a vocational and technical training framework, building new skills and innovative thinking, not only for existing jobs but also jobs that are to be created. Improving the skill development of students in higher education would contribute substantially to placing higher education as the foremost pillar on which our society is built. The academic world has serious doubts about where our society is going in many respects. However, the students going through higher education become the citizens who determine the nature of our society. Thus, higher education has a crucial opportunity to affect the future of our society through substantially improving the skill development of our citizens.

Introduction

Skill Development efforts across the country have been highly fragmented so far. Though India enjoys the demographic advantage of having the youngest workforce with an average age of 29 years in comparison with the advanced economies, as opposed to the developed countries, where the percentage of skilled workforce is between 60% and 90% of the total workforce, India records a low 5% of workforce (20-24 years) with formal employability skills. With the present education and skill levels of those already in the labour force being very low, it would be a major challenge for India to reap its demographic advantage.

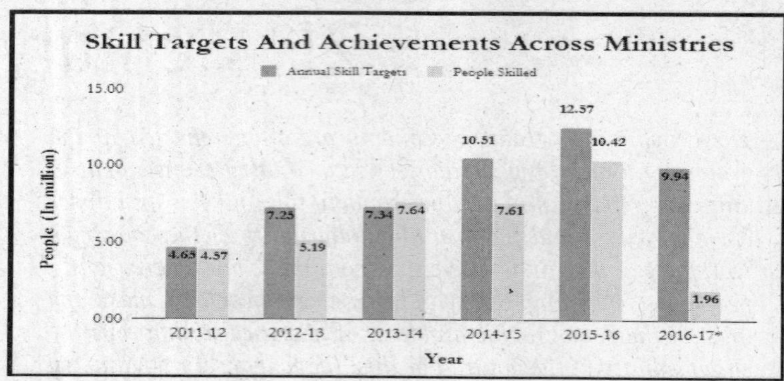

Source: National Skill development agency annual report 2016.

Education and Skill Development

India is on the threshold of a demographic dividend—a dividend that is waiting to be reaped. For this dividend to be meaningful however, education, the basic right to which is now guaranteed by the constitution of India, needs to be supplemented with a skill development strategy that can ensure gainful employment.

Skill Training interventions raises confidence, improves productivity & competency of an individual through focussed outcome based learning.

❖ Skills at School Level

At school level, there must be options available for skill development courses and they must be provided in the secondary stage of schooling. Many more courses in fields such as Hospitality and Tourism, Handicraft, Healthcare, Textiles, Photography, IT, Retail, Banking, Insurance can be added that would interest students to learn from skill development courses. For instance if a student opts for healthcare, he/she could learn to be a blood-collection specialist and later can pursue further courses to become full-fledged pathology technician or nurse.

The pedagogy should focus on learning by practical means; it suggests that learning can be enhanced through field visits, e-learning, industry driven projects, digital or video inputs and so on. Skill development should ideally begin at the age of 13 years, from the eighth standard, while in school.

Integration of skill development and education is essential for improving skills. Skill development will remain a dream if carried out in isolation through centers alone. It has to be imparted in schools alongside academics.

If a student opts for motor repair as a skill development course while in school; at a later stage, he can opt for a diploma or degree in automobile engineering. These are some of the practicable skills that should be introduced to school students from an early age of 6-7 years onwards in an incremental manner:

- Primary school (classes 1 to 5) (age 6 to 11): Communication skills, attitude, adaptability and IT skills
- Middle school (classes 6 to 8) (age 11 to 14): Above skills plus self-management, teamwork, creativity
- Secondary education (classes 9 to 10) (age 14 to 15): Above skills plus stress management, self-motivation
- Upper secondary (classes 11 to 12) (age 16 to 17): Above skills plus initiative, interpersonal sensitivity

- Higher education (graduation or professional programmes): Above skills plus commercial awareness, problem solving, lifelong learning.

❖ Skills at college level

In the higher education sphere knowledge and skills are required for a diversity of employment needs in the services, education, health care, and manufacturing sector etc. Potentially, the target group for skill development comprises all those in the labour force, including those entering the labour market for the first time, those employed in the organized sector and those working in the unorganized sector.

In an attempt to integrate skill based trainings into the academic cycle of the Universities, National Skill Development Corporation (NSDC) has made a unique model. The following points are based on the model developed by NSDC:

- Identification of Sectors and job roles
- Development of implementation model and Integration into time table as per university norms
- Training of Trainers by Sector Skill Council
- Curriculum Alignment and Capacity Building workshops
- Student orientation sessions to take an informed choice of sector/job role based on career aspiration
- Standardised Training Delivery by NSDC Training Partners
- Internships and On- the – job Training
- Assessment and certification by Sector Skill Council
- Last Mile Employability and Entrepreneurship Opportunities for the students

❖ Skills at university level

With the world of work changing fast, and a growing need for higher level skills, universities have a crucial role to play. For this purpose as per the National Policy for Skill Development & Entrepreneurship, 2015—"National Skills Universities and Institutes will be promoted in partnership with States as centres of excellence for skill development and training of trainers, either as de-novo institutions or as a part of existing university landscape.

Skills Universities—conceived and constructed with a clear mandate for skills education would create a parallel vocational counterpart to general education. Such universities shall cater to the national and international job markets across sectors. Through such network of Skills Universities, skills based education will acquire aspirational value and social acceptability in the society and the economy.

Skills Universities will fill the long pending need for higher level institutions in the Skills space and would help harvest latent value in India's existing skills landscape.

Education without Skills is not Useful

While education is important, it does not guarantee us a job in our chosen field. One learns a lot of theories during foundational education, but applying them to practical work requires skills which, for the most part, are not taught as part of the degree programme. For example, the recent studies indicate that employers found just about 25% of Indian graduates are 'employable' in the organized sector. The informal sector which comprises 93% of the workforce has no skilling mechanism, as the skill development takes place on the job.

Difference between Knowledge and Skills

Knowledge is information acquired through sensory input: Reading, watching, listening, touching, etc. The concept of knowledge refers to familiarity with factual information and theoretical concepts.

Skills, however, refer to the ability to apply knowledge to specific situations. Skills are developed through practice, through a combination of sensory input and output.

As an example, an aerospace engineer may know a lot about avionics and flight theory, but this alone does not make him an aircraft pilot. On the other end, an aircraft pilot only requires a minimal level of knowledge about avionics and flight theory in order to be able to fly the plane, and this knowledge will continue to increase as he gains experience flying a simulator or an actual plane.

Skills and Jobs

Unfortunately, a university degree may well be insufficient. It is skills and experiences that can make you a desired applicant and supplement your qualifications. Skill based learning focuses on increasing employability through series of inputs to equip students with appropriate hands-on skills which helps them to be job-ready.

According to the fifth edition of the Confederation of Indian Industry's (CII) 'India Skills Report 2018', this year's employability score reached a new level of 45.60 percent, which is 5.16 percent more than the last year's score. The score suggests that about five out of 10 graduates are employable and are ready to jump into jobs. A rising score is reflective of the efforts undertaken by various stakeholders, including the government.

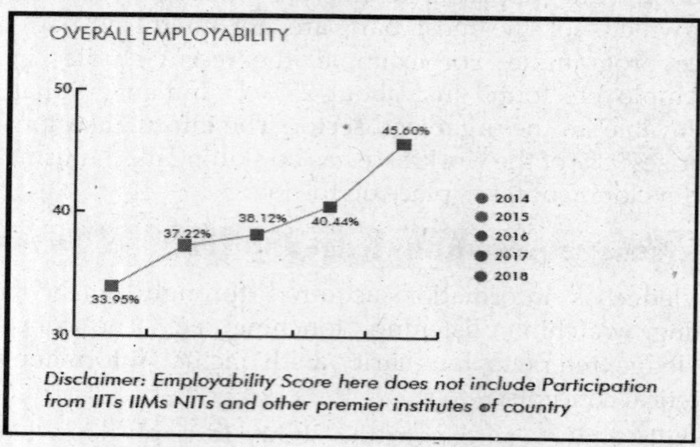

And also there is a substantial increase in the number of people who were skilled in FY17 and FY18. It has risen more than four times, from over 3.5 lakh people in FY17 to nearly 16 lakh people in FY18. But not everyone who is getting skilled is getting placed.

In FY17 just over half of those skilled managed to find jobs and in FY18 this fell below 30%, meaning just about 3 out of every 10 persons who undertook the Skill India mission in FY18 found a job. So there is a 4-fold increase in those getting trained but only a 2-fold increase in those finding jobs.

❖ Sector wise data from RTI petition on PMKY 2015–16

Agriculture, the largest contributor to GDP saw a 2-fold rise in those trained but placements were not forthcoming. Only 37% found jobs in FY18.

Labour intensive sectors like leather saw a drop in the number of people who got skilled and those who found jobs. Over 5,400 people were trained in FY17 in leather sector but this dropped to about 3,000 in FY18. Moreover, only 42% of those skilled found jobs in FY18 in the sector.

In the textiles space, the number of people trained in FY18 compared to FY17 has halved and only 55% found jobs in FY18.

In capital goods there is an almost 5-fold jump in the number of people trained from FY17 to FY18 but only 23% found a job in FY18. Leather, textiles and capital goods are all export-driven sectors and jobs are scarce in all three of them, clearly indicating the state of the economy.

Two sectors where the government has made a big push for training and developing skills has been electronics and IT.

In electronics, there is an 11-fold rise in the number of people trained from FY17 to FY18. But, there is only a 5-fold increase in jobs with 25% of those trained finding placements in FY18.

The IT industry is mirroring the electronics sector where once again there is an 11-fold increase in those getting trained but only 2 out of 10 trained in this sector found a job.

A recent report from research agency Crisil also alluded to this point. "Labour-light sectors have expanded faster than labour intensive ones over the last few years. Thus, the faster-growing sectors have offered fewer employment opportunities. This trend intensified in fiscals 2017 and 2018, when the economy was in the throes of a slowdown."

Skill Development and Economic Development

Knowledge and skills would increasingly become the primary determinants of economic growth and development and countries with higher and better levels of skills will adjust more effectively to the challenges and opportunities of growth in a globalised world.

Skills and knowledge are driving forces of economic growth and social development for any country. Countries with higher levels and better standards of skills adjust more effectively to the challenges and opportunities in domestic and international job markets.

First, India has struggled with defining the role and importance of skill development in national growth. In fact, according to the India Economic Survey 2017 by the Organisation of Economic Cooperation & Development (OECD), public spending on education in India is 3.8% of the GDP. The education system and syllabus haven't kept up with the fast-changing business needs, especially those that are interlinked to soft skills, advanced technology adoption, and even the flexibility to re-skill for emerging opportunities.

Second, the job creation itself has been low, and in this context, the OECD Survey highlights the complex labor laws, limited quality jobs, and restrictive employment protection legislation in the Indian market. Each of these factors acts as a deterrent to the successful employment of India's labor force.

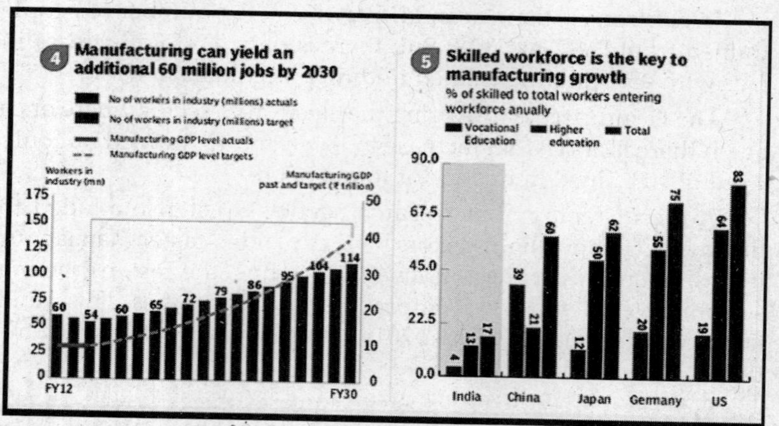

Source: Financial Express

Skills for 21st Century

21st Century skills are 12 abilities that today's students need to succeed in their careers during the Information Age.

These skills are intended to help students keep up with the lightning-pace of today's modern markets. Each skill is unique in how it helps students, but they all have one quality in common.

Critical thinking: In business settings, critical thinking is essential to improvement. It's the mechanism that weeds out problems and replaces them with fruitful endeavours.

Creativity is equally important as a means of adaptation. This skill empowers students to see concepts in a different light, which leads to innovation.

Collaboration means getting students to work together, achieve compromises, and get the best possible results from solving a problem.

Finally, **communication** is the glue that brings all of these educational qualities together.

Communication is a requirement for any company to maintain profitability. It's crucial for students to learn how to effectively convey ideas among different personality types.

Information literacy is the foundational skill. It helps students understand facts, especially data points that they'll encounter online.

In an age of chronic misinformation, finding truth online has become a job all on its own. It's crucial that students can identify honesty on their own.

Media literacy is the practice of identifying publishing methods, outlets, and sources while distinguishing between the ones that are credible and the ones that aren't.

Just like the previous skill, media literacy is helpful for finding truth in a world that's saturated with information.

Technology literacy goes another step further to teach students about the machines involved in the Information Age.

Technology literacy gives students the basic information they need to understand what gadgets perform what tasks and why.

Flexibility is the expression of someone's ability to adapt to changing circumstances. This is one of the most challenging qualities to learn for students because it's based on two uncomfortable ideas:

- Your way isn't always the best way
- You have to know and admit when you're wrong

Leadership is someone's penchant for setting goals, walking a team through the steps required, and achieving those goals collaboratively.

Entry-level workers need leadership skills for several reasons. The most important is that it helps them understand the decisions that managers and business leaders make.

Initiative only comes naturally to a handful of people. As a result, students need to learn it to fully succeed.

This is one of the hardest skills to learn and practice. Initiative often means working on projects outside of regular working hours.

Productivity: Along with initiative, 21st Century skills require students to learn about productivity. That's a student's ability to complete work in an appropriate amount of time.

By understanding productivity strategies at every level, students discover the ways in which they work best while gaining an appreciation for how others work as well.

Social skills are crucial to the ongoing success of a professional. Business is frequently done through the connections one person makes with others around them.

This concept of networking is more active in some industries than others, but proper social skills are excellent tools for forging long-lasting relationships.

How to Impart These Skills

The "Singapore Swiss Roll" approach, which is starting to be implemented across the core curriculum, adopts a value-centric framework that incorporates 21st century competencies, including civic literacy, global awareness, and cross-cultural skills; critical and inventive thinking; communication, collaboration and information skills; as well as social and emotional competencies.

Australia's national curriculum of 2010 identified seven general capabilities, which teachers are expected to integrate throughout their teaching. They are guided by online resources provided by the Australian Curriculum Assessment and Reporting Authority.

❖ Way Forward

Economic development, employment and skills related initiatives can cross-fertilise and nurture synergies for the benefit of the local community if they are well co-ordinated. Yet, they are often managed separately. As a result, slow population growth and an ageing workforce generate skills shortages and hinder business growth, while many low-skilled workers remain stuck at the bottom of the labour market, representing an untapped resource for the economy. So the focus was on how these employment, skills and economic development policy areas could generally be better integrated to maximise benefits for the economy and society, as well as to foster business development, and the enhancement of skills and social inclusion.

With the Fourth Industrial Revolution round the corner, it needs to be ensured that our youth thrives any shift in the skill requirements in both foundational soft skills and skills specific to different job roles. The real success of Skill India Mission will not be when all are skilled, but when all skilled find relevant jobs. Hence, an equal push needs to be creating jobs.

❑❑❑

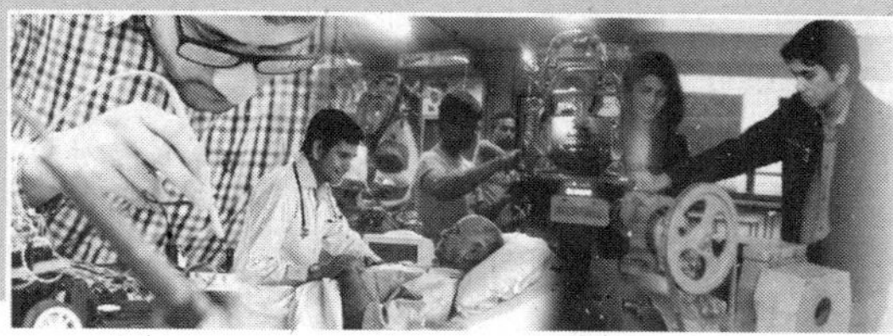

Chapter

2

Skill India – Kaushal Bharat - Kushal Bharat

Introduction

"Let's make India the Skill Capital of the world"

Skills and knowledge are driving forces of economic growth and social development for any country. Countries with higher levels and better standards of skills adjust more effectively to the challenges and opportunities in domestic and international job markets. The country, however, has a big challenge ahead as it is estimated that only 4.69% of the total workforce in India has undergone formal skill training. India currently holds the distinction for being one of the youngest nations in the world, i.e. largest youth demography.

According to a report by the Ministry of Skill Development and Entrepreneurship, over 54% of India's total population is below 25 years of age, and over 62% of the population comes under the working age group (15-59 years). It also predicts that our country's population pyramid is expected to swell across the stated working age over the next decade. Thus, it has now become a matter of extreme importance for India to utilize its demographic dividend and overcome the Skills gap within a limited timeline.

Skill Development Statistics

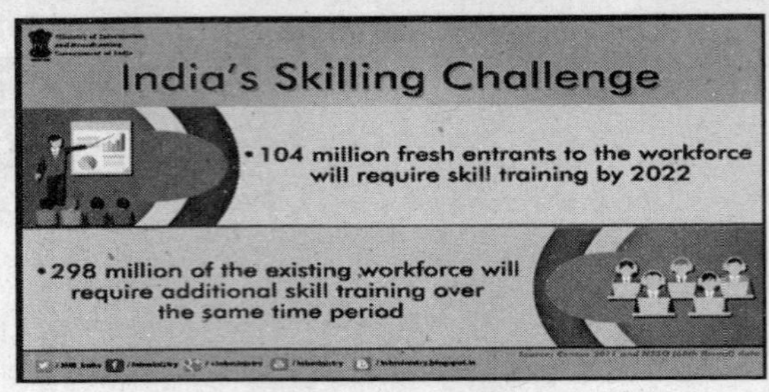

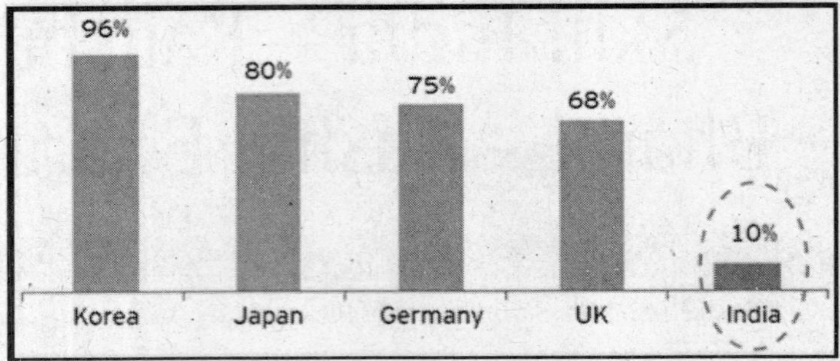

Source: Planning Commission

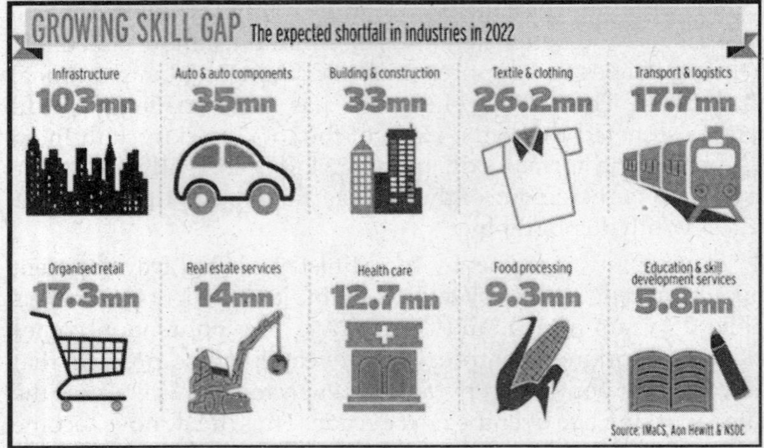

❖ Challenges for SKILL INDIA

There exists several challenges in the skilling and entrepreneurship landscape in the country; a few of the many are enumerated below:

- Public perception that views skilling as the last option meant for those who have not been able to progress/ opted out of the formal academic system.
- Skill development programmes of the Central Government are spread across more than 18 Ministries/ Departments without any robust coordination and monitoring mechanism to ensure convergence. For example, min of labour and employment, min of HRD, NSDC has been setting up their own sector skill councils.
- Multiplicity in assessment and certification systems that leads to inconsistent outcomes and causes confusion among the employers.
- Paucity of trainers, inability to attract practitioners from industry as faculty
- Mismatch between demand and supply at the sectoral and spatial levels
- Limited mobility between skill and higher education programs and vocational education
- Very low coverage, poorly designed apprenticeship programs devoid of industry linkages
- Narrow and often obsolete skill curricula and existing training infra is irrelevant to industry needs.
- Declining labour force participation rate of women
- Pre-dominant non-farm, unorganized sector employment with low productivity but no premium for skilling
- Non-inclusion of entrepreneurship in formal education system
- Lack of mentorship and adequate access to finance for startups
- Inadequate impetus to innovation driven entrepreneurship
- Private sector offers less % of formal training when compared to other nations.

❖ Advantages of Skill India

The idea is to raise confidence, improve productivity and give direction through proper skill development. Skill development will enable the youth to get blue-collar jobs. Development of skills, at a young age, right at the school level, is very essential to channelise them for proper job opportunities. There should be a balanced growth in all the sectors and all jobs should be given equal importance. Every job aspirant would be given training in soft skills to lead a proper and decent life. Skill development would reach the rural and remote areas also. Corporate educational institutions, non-government organizations, Government, academic institutions, and society would help in the development of skills of the youths so that better results are achieved in the shortest time possible.

Policy Interventions

National Policy for Skill Development & Entrepreneurship, 2015:

❖ Vision Statement

"To create an ecosystem of empowerment by skilling on a large scale at speed with high standards and to promote a culture of innovation based entrepreneurship which can generate wealth and employment so as to ensure Sustainable Livelihoods for all citizens in the Country."

❖ Skill Component of Policy

The skill component of the Policy addresses key issues in the skill landscape: low aspirational value, non-integration with formal education, lack of focus on outcomes, quality of training infrastructure and trainers - among others. The Policy aims to align supply with demand, bridge existing skill gaps, promote industry engagement, operationalise a quality assurance framework, leverage technology and promote apprenticeship to tackle the identified issues. It also aims to promote equitable skilling opportunities for socially/geographically marginalised and disadvantaged groups as well as women.

❖ Entrepreneurship Component of Policy

In the entrepreneurship domain, the Policy seeks to promote entrepreneurial culture through advocacy and integration of entrepreneurship education as part of formal/skill education, enhance support for entrepreneurs in terms of credit and market linkages, foster innovation driven and social enterprises and improve ease of doing business. It also suggests ways to further fillip entrepreneurship among women besides endeavoring to meet the entrepreneurial needs of socially/geographically marginalized and disadvantaged groups.

National Skill Development Mission: National Skill Development Mission aims to create convergence and expedite cross-sectoral decisions through a high powered decision making framework. It is expected to converge, coordinate, implement and monitor skilling activities on a pan-India basis.

The Mission consists of a three tier institutional structure, where the cascading functions of the bodies consist of providing policy directives and guidance, reviewing and monitoring overall progress, and actual implementation in line with Mission objectives. The Mission will also run select sub-missions in high priority areas. The power to identify sub-missions would lie with the Governing Council. At the outset, seven sub-missions have been proposed in the following areas:

1. Institutional Training
2. Infrastructure
3. Convergence
4. Trainers
5. Overseas Employment
6. Sustainable Livelihoods
7. Leveraging Public Infrastructure

National Board for Skills Assessment and Certification

Assessment processes in the country so far have been highly fragmented and varied. Poor regulation procedures and non-uniformity in assessment guidelines has called the entire skill assessment ecosystem into question.

The Ministry is working on a concept for a National Board for Skills Assessment and Certification which will bring together the industry-led SSC certification processes and government authorized NCVT certification.

The Board will act as a one stop shop for examinations, assessments and awarding national level certificates in compliance with National Skills Qualification Framework (NSQF) for skill development courses in the country.

A budget of ₹ 25 Cr has been allocated of FY 2017-18 to set up the Board as an autonomous organization and ensure that the skills assessment ecosystem in the country is maintained at a high standard.

National Skills Qualifications Framework (NSQF)

The National Skills Qualifications Framework (NSQF) is a competency-based framework that organizes all qualifications according to a series of levels of knowledge, skills and aptitude. These levels, graded from one to ten, are defined in terms of learning outcomes which the learner must possess regardless of whether they are obtained through formal, non-formal or informal learning. NSQF in India was notified on 27th December 2013. All other frameworks, including the NVEQF (National Vocational Educational Qualification Framework) released by the Ministry of HRD, stand superceded by the NSQF.

Under NSQF, the learner can acquire the certification for competency needed at any level through formal, non-formal or informal learning. In that sense, the NSQF is a quality assurance framework. Presently, more than 100 countries have, or are in the process of developing national qualification frameworks.

The NSQF is anchored at the National Skill Development Agency (NSDA) and is being implemented through the National Skills Qualifications Committee (NSQC) which comprises of all key stakeholders. The NSQC's functions amongst others include approving NOSs/QPs, approving accreditation norms, prescribing guidelines to address the needs of disadvantaged sections, reviewing inter-agency disputes and alignment of NSQF with international qualification frameworks.

Specific outcomes expected from implementation of NSQF are:

- Mobility between vocational and general education by alignment of degrees with NSQF
- Recognition of Prior Learning (RPL), allowing transition from non-formal to organised job market

- Standardised, consistent, nationally acceptable outcomes of training across the country through a national quality assurance framework
- Global mobility of skilled workforce from India, through international equivalence of NSQF
- Mapping of progression pathways within sectors and cross-sectorally
- Approval of NOS/QPs as national standards for skill training

Sector Skill Councils

Sector Skill Councils (SSCs) are set up as autonomous bodies and Not-for-Profit organizations by the National Skill Development Corporation and are led by industry leaders in respective sectors. They create Occupational Standards, develop competency framework, conduct Train the Trainer Programs, affiliate Vocational Training Institutes, conduct skill gap studies in their sector leading to a Labor Market Information System and most importantly Assess and Certify trainees on the curriculum aligned to National Occupational Standards developed by them.

Sector Skill Councils are designed to be national partnership organizations that bring together all the stakeholders – industry, labor and academia. As on date 40 Sector Skill Councils are approved covering all the priority and high growth sectors like Automotive, Retail, Healthcare, Leather, Food Processing, etc. and informal sectors like Beauty & Wellness, Security, Domestic Workers & Plumbing. The list includes 20 High Priority Sectors identified by the Government and 25 of the sectors under make in India.

Government Schemes

❖ SKILL INDIA

Objectives

The main goal is to create opportunities, space and scope for the development of the talents of the Indian youth and to develop more of those sectors which have already been put under skill development for the last so many years and also to identify new sectors for skill development. The new programme aims at providing training and skill development to 500 million youth of our country by 2020, covering each and every village. Various schemes are also proposed to achieve this objective.

Features

The emphasis is to skill the youths in such a way so that they get employment and also improve entrepreneurship.

Provides training, support and guidance for all occupations that were of traditional type like carpenters, cobblers, welders, blacksmiths, masons, nurses, tailors, weavers etc.

More emphasis will be given on new areas like real estate, construction, transportation, textile, gem industry, jewellery designing, banking, tourism and various other sectors, where skill development is inadequate or nil.

The training programmes would be on the lines of international level so that the youths of our country can not only meet the domestic demands but also of other countries like the US, Japan, China, Germany, Russia and those in the West Asia. Another remarkable feature of the 'Skill India' programme would be to create a hallmark called 'Rural India Skill', so as to standardise and certify the training process.

Tailor-made, need-based programmes would be initiated for specific age groups which can be like language and communication skills, life and positive thinking skills, personality development skills, management skills, behavioural skills, including job and employability skills.

The course methodology of 'Skill India' would be innovative, which would include games, group discussions, brainstorming sessions, practical experiences, case studies etc

Pradhan Mantri Kaushal Vikas Yojana (PMKVY)

Pradhan Mantri Kaushal Vikas Yojana (PMKVY) is the flagship scheme of the Ministry of Skill Development & Entrepreneurship (MSDE). The objective of this Skill Certification Scheme is to enable a large number of Indian youth to take up industry-relevant skill training that will help them in securing a better livelihood. Individuals with prior learning experience or skills will also be assessed and certified under Recognition of Prior Learning (RPL). Under this Scheme, Training and Assessment fees are completely paid by the Government.

❖ Key Components of the Scheme

1. Short Term Training

The Short Term Training imparted at PMKVY Training Centres (TCs) is expected to benefit candidates of Indian nationality who are either school/college dropouts or unemployed. Apart from providing training according to the National Skills Qualification Framework (NSQF), TCs shall also impart training in Soft Skills, Entrepreneurship, Financial and Digital Literacy. Duration of the training varies per job role, ranging between 150 and 300 hours. Upon successful completion of their assessment, candidates shall be provided placement assistance by Training Partners (TPs). Under PMKVY, the entire training and assessment fees is paid by the Government. Payouts shall be provided to the TPs in alignment with the Common Norms. Trainings imparted under the Short Term Training component of the Scheme shall be NSQF Level 5 and below.

2. Recognition of prior learning

Individuals with prior learning experience or skills shall be assessed and certified under the Recognition of Prior Learning (RPL) component of the Scheme. RPL aims to align the competencies of the unregulated workforce of the country to the NSQF. Project Implementing Agencies (PIAs), such as Sector Skill Councils (SSCs) or any other agencies designated by MSDE/NSDC, shall be incentivized to implement RPL projects in any of the three Project Types (RPL Camps, RPL at Employers Premises and RPL centres). To address knowledge gaps, PIAs may offer Bridge Courses to RPL candidates.

3. Special Projects

The Special Projects component of PMKVY envisages the creation of a platform that will facilitate trainings in special areas and/or premises of Government bodies, Corporates or Industry bodies, and trainings in special job roles not defined under the available Qualification Packs (QPs)/National Occupational Standards

(NOSs). Special Projects are projects that require some deviation from the terms and conditions of Short Term Training under PMKVY for any stakeholder. A proposing stakeholder can be either Government Institutions of Central and State Government(s)/ Autonomous Body/Statutory Body or any other equivalent body or corporates who desire to provide training to candidates.

4. Kaushal and Rozgar Mela

Social and community mobilisation is extremely critical for the success of PMKVY. Active participation of the community ensures transparency and accountability, and helps in leveraging the cumulative knowledge of the community for better functioning. In line with this, PMKVY assigns special importance to the involvement of the target beneficiaries through a defined mobilisation process. TPs shall conduct Kaushal and Rozgar Melas every six months with press/media coverage; they are also required to participate actively in National Career Service Melas and on-ground activities.

5. Placement Guidelines

PMKVY envisages to link the aptitude, aspiration, and knowledge of the skilled workforce it creates with employment opportunities and demands in the market. Every effort thereby needs to be made by the PMKVY TCs to provide placement opportunities to candidates, trained and certified under the Scheme. TPs shall also provide support to entrepreneurship development.

6. Monitoring Guidelines

To ensure that high standards of quality are maintained by PMKVY TCs, NSDC and empaneled Inspection Agencies shall use various methodologies, such as self-audit reporting, call validations, surprise visits, and monitoring through the Skills Development Management System (SDMS). These methodologies shall be enhanced with the engagement of latest technologies.

The scheme will be implemented through the National Skill Development Corporation (NSDC).

UDAAN

Udaan is a Special Industry Initiative for Jammu & Kashmir in the nature of partnership between the corporates of India and

Ministry of Home Affairs and implemented by National Skill Development Corporation. The programme aims to provide skills training and enhance the employability of unemployed youth of J&K. The Scheme covers graduates, post graduates and three year engineering diploma holders. It has two objectives:

1. To provide an exposure to the unemployed graduates to the best of Corporate India;
2. To provide Corporate India, an exposure to the rich talent pool available in the State.

The key stakeholders are:

- Ministry of Home Affairs (MHA) - Chief Benefactors
- State Government (Jammu & Kashmir)
- Corporates - Training Partners
- Implementation Agency (IA) NSDC

The Scheme aims to cover 40,000 youth of J&K over a period of five years and ₹ 750 crore has been earmarked for implementation of the scheme over a period of five years to cover other incidental expenses such as travel cost, boarding and lodging, stipend and travel and medical insurance cost for the trainees and administration cost. Further corporates are eligible for partial reimbursement of training expense incurred for the candidates who have been offered jobs.

❖ Pradhan Mantri Kaushal Kendra (PMKK)

Vocational training needs to be made aspirational to transform India into the skill capital of the world. In line with the same, Ministry of Skill Development and Entrepreneurship (MSDE) intends to establish visible and aspirational Model Training Centres (MTCs) in every district of the country. NSDC is the implementation agency for the project. These training centres will be state-of-the-art Model Training Centres, called as Pradhan Mantri Kaushal Kendra (PMKK).

Objectives

The model training centres envisage to:

- Create benchmark institutions that demonstrate aspirational value for competency-based skill development training.

- Focus on elements of quality, sustainability and Connection with stakeholders in skills delivery process.
- Transform from a Mandate-driven footloose model to a sustainable institutional model.

❖ PRAVASI KAUSHAL VIKAS YOJANA

Pravasi Kaushal Vikas Yojana (PKVY) is to enhance skills of youth in line with the international standards and help them getting overseas employment. Similar to Pradhan Mantri Kaushal Vikas Yojana (PMKVY), it will be implemented by the National Skill Development Corporation (NSDC) through its training Partners and in Consultation with the Union Ministry of External Affairs and the Union Skill Development Ministry.

Key Components of the Scheme

PKVY is aimed at imparting skills to Indian youth, who is seeking employment in overseas. PKVY is launched as a means of showing respect to the Indians, who is living overseas by ensuring their Welfare and Safety.

The short term program (of 2 weeks to one month) will prepare the candidates holistically in taking up challenging assignments in different countries with confidence and meet transnational skill requirements.

The program could be of great help to blue collar workers who get an opportunity to acquire professional skills and be able to communicate in the foreign language, besides getting skilled in particular trades.

It also aims at boosting the confidence of the Indian youth so that they don't feel like strangers when they land in a country of their choice for vocation.

Key International Engagements

1. **United Kingdom:** An MoU was signed between MSDE and the UK Department of Business Innovation and Skills (BIS) in April 2015. Key areas of collaboration were identified and a number of workshops, exchange visits and training programmes have already taken place under UKIERI II. In addition, collaborations have been initiated with over 15 Indian Sector Skill Councils and their UK counterparts to benchmark Indian training standards with UK standards.

UKIERI II ended on 31 March 2015. MSDE has joined the UKIERI III initiative for institutional partnerships in Skills, developing occupational standards, technology enabled training, apprenticeship and employer engagement and sharing of best practices between UK and India.

2. **Germany:** MSDE participated in the Hannover Messe in April 2015 and set up the Skill Pavilion. In October 2015, an MoU was signed between the two countries to collaborate in a number of areas which included: scaling up workplace based training in industrial clusters, training of trainers, upgradation of curricula, upgradation of existing institutions etc. Roadmap for the way forward has been agreed on by the two sides and joint activities have started.
3. **Australia:** NSDC is working with many Australian institutions to operationalise this collaboration. An MoU was signed between NSDC and TAFE SA and Heraud in January 2015 for establishing a centre of excellence. A study tour to Australia was organized for key officials working on skills training to understand Australia's skills ecosystem and document lessons for India.
4. **Canada:** NSDC signed 13 MoUs with some of Canada's key skill training institutions, during the Hon'ble Prime Minister of India's visit to Canada in April 2015. The MoUs are focused on sharing best practices, international recognition of standards and creating new Centres for Excellence in India.
5. **European Union:** An MoU was signed between Department of Economic Affairs, Ministry of Finance and EU in June 2014 for implementation of the skill development policy of GOI. A number of capacity building activities have been undertaken within this India-EU skills development project. A number of study tours, delegation visits, training of trainers, assessors etc have taken place through this collaboration. This project was completed in January 2017.
6. **France:** MoU between NSDA and CNCP (Commission Nationale de la Certification Professionnelle – CNCP), France was signed on January 2015 to understand the knowledge base of developing and implementing the Qualification Register in France and India. Exchange visit was undertaken by CNCP representative to India and NSDA representatives to France under this collaboration.

WAY FORWARD

The benefits of a growing economy are often reflected in the growing number of well-paid jobs in a country. Consequently, any policy that stimulates the economy to grow has an impact on job creation and the overall employability of the country's workforce. India finds itself in a context today where young people are entering the workforce every year. To make the most of the demographic dividend, it is critical to improve the employability of the youth. For this, the newly set up Ministry of Skill Development and Entrepreneurship had taken up the task of coordinating all skill development efforts across the country. This includes the removal of the disconnect between demand and supply of skilled manpower, building a vocational and technical training framework, building new skills and innovative thinking, not only for existing jobs but also jobs that are to be created.

To achieve this task, following measures are needed to be taken:

- delivery of atleast 70% of total skill development targets should rest solely with MSDE,
- Directorate general of employment and training should be integrated with MSDE,
- MSDE must explicitly be made responsible for coordination with the states and their skill development missions.
- Improve resource utilization, scientific monitoring and evaluation methods need to be incorporated in every program to ensure just utilization of resources.
- Development of a fully functional labour market information system that can provide an accurate statistical base for formulating and monitoring vocational training policies and programmes.
- Engaging the private sector, for any skill development effort to succeed, markets and industry need to play a large role in determining courses, curriculum and relevance.
- The government has its task cutout. What is needed is a willingness to act and to take the difficult decisions that can help realize the SKILL INDIA dream and making India the SKILL CAPITAL OF THE WORLD.

❑❑❑

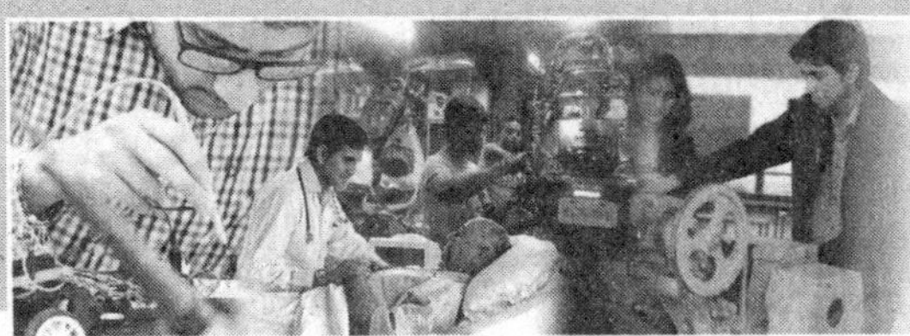

Chapter

3

Skill Development: An Introductory Overview

Introduction

Skill is the ability to execute a task with pre-determined results often within the tight deadline of time and energy. Skills are generally of two types: Domain general and domain-specific management. For instance, in the field of work, some general skills are time management, teamwork and leadership, self-motivation and others; whereas domain-specific skills are only for a particular job. Skill usually requires specific environment where inspiration and situations are helpful to assess the level of skill being shown and applied. People require diverse skills in order to contribute to the modern economy.

- ***Labour Skills:*** Skilled workers such as bakers, blacksmiths, brewers, carpenters, coopers, printers, electricians, masons and others have traditionally imported setup. They were often politically active through their cooperation and association.
- ***Life Skills:*** Life skills comprise of problem-solving behaviours. People use them responsibly and accurately in managing personal affairs. Life skills are a unit of human skills that people acquire by means of learning or practical experience by handling the day-to-day problems and situations in everyday life. The

subject varies completely based on the norms of the society and expectations of the community.

- ***People Skills:*** The Portland Business Journal explains 'people skills' as understanding ourselves and moderating our responses; talking effectively and empathizing accurately; and building relationships of trust, respect, and productive interactions. However, a British definition is "the ability to communicate effectively with people in a friendly way, especially in business." The term 'people skills' includes psychological skills and social skills, but it is less comprehensive than life skills.
- ***Social Skills:*** Social skill is any skill that helps to interact and communicate with others. The rules and relations of society are created, communicated verbally and nonverbally.
- ***Soft Skills:*** It is a sociological term relating to a person's 'EQ' (Emotional Intelligence Quotient). The collections of personality traits, social graces, communication, language, personal habits, friendliness and optimism are soft skills that indicate relationships with other people. Soft skills supplement hard skills (part of a person's IQ) integral to the professional and many other activities.
- ***Hard Skills***: Hard skills, essential to specific works or situations, are easily measurable unlike soft skills relating to one's personality.

Select Examples of Skills

❖ **Examples of job skills**

- Ability to Work under Pressure
- Accuracy
- Adaptability
- Administering Medication
- Advising People
- Analysing Data
- Analysing Problems
- Assembling Equipment
- Attention to Detail

- Auditing Financial Data
- Analytical Skills
- Attention to Details
- Being Thorough
- Brainstorming
- Budgeting
- Building New Business
- Business Communication Skills
- Business Management Skills
- Calculating Data
- Categorizing Records
- Checking for Accuracy
- Coaching Skills
- Collaborating Ideas
- Collecting Items
- Communicating with Young or Old People
- Comparing Results
- Comprehending Books or Ideas
- Conducting Interviews
- Conflict Resolution
- Confronting other People
- Constructing Buildings
- Consulting Organizations
- Counselling People
- Creative Thinking Skills
- Creating Meaningful Work
- Critical Thinking Skills
- Customer Service Skills
- Dealing with Complaints
- Decision Making Skills
- Defining Problems
- Delegating Skills
- Designing Systems

- Determination
- Developing Plans for Projects
- Diplomacy Skills
- Displaying Art
- Distributing Products
- Dramatizing Ideas
- Driving Safely
- Editing
- Effective Listening Skills
- Effective Study Skills
- Encouraging People
- Enforcing Rules
- Entertaining Others
- Envisioning Solutions or Ideas
- Estimating Project Workload
- Ethics
- Evaluating Programs
- Expressing Feelings
- Expressing Ideas
- Extracting Information
- Finding Missing Information
- Following Instructions
- Gathering Information
- Generating Accounts
- Goal Setting
- Initiator
- Handling Money
- Identifying Problems
- Imagining Innovative Solutions
- Information Management
- Inspecting Buildings
- Inspecting Equipment
- Interacting with Various People

- Interpersonal Communication Skills
- Interpreting Languages
- Interviewing
- Inventing Products/Ideas
- Investigating Solutions
- Knowledge of Community
- Knowledge of Concepts and Principles
- Knowledge of Government Affairs
- Leading Teams
- Listening to People
- Maintain Focus with Interruptions
- Maintaining a High Level of Production
- Maintaining Accurate Records
- Maintaining Emotional Control under Stress
- Maintaining Files
- Maintaining Schedules or Timings
- Making Important Decisions
- Managing Organizations
- Managing People
- Mediating between People
- Meeting Deadlines
- Meeting New People
- Motivating Others
- Multi-Tasking
- Navigating Politics
- Negotiating Skills
- Operating Equipment
- Organizing Files
- Organizing Tasks
- Patience
- People Management Skills
- Performing Clerical Work
- Performing Numerical Analysis

- Persuading Others
- Planning Meetings
- Planning Organizational Needs
- Predicting Future Trends
- Preparing Written Communications
- Prioritization Skills
- Problem Analysis Skills
- Problem Solving Skills
- Product Promotion
- Promoting Events
- Proposing Ideas
- Providing Customer Service
- Providing Discipline
- Public Speaking
- Questioning Others
- Quick Learning Skills
- Raising Funds
- Reading
- Recognizing Problems
- Recruiting
- Rehabilitating People
- Relating to Others
- Reliability
- Remembering Information
- Repairing Equipment
- Reporting Data
- Researching
- Resolving Conflicts
- Resourcefulness
- Responsibility
- Results Orientated
- Risk Taking
- Running Meetings

- Sales Ability
- Screening Telephone Calls
- Self-Motivated
- Selling Ideas
- Selling Products or Services
- Serving People
- Setting Performance Standards
- Setting up Demonstrations
- Sketching Charts or Diagrams
- Strategic Thinking
- Suggesting Courses of Action
- Summarizing Data
- Supervising Employees
- Supervising Operations
- Supporting Others
- Taking Decisive Action
- Taking Initiative
- Taking Personal Responsibility
- Teaching Skills
- Team Building
- Teamwork Skills
- Technical Work
- Thinking Logically
- Time Management Skills
- Training Skills
- Translating Words
- Using Computers
- Verbal Communication Skills
- Working Creatively
- Working with Statistics
- Writing Clearly and Concisely
- Writing Letters, Papers, or Proposals

❖ Examples of Life Skills

- Baking
- Canning or preserving
- Changing a tire on a car
- Changing a light bulb
- Checking the oil in a car
- Cleaning your residence
- Clearing a drain
- Clearing the table
- Cooking
- Cardiopulmonary Resuscitation
- Driving
- Drying clothes and dishes
- Dusting furniture
- First Aid
- Folding clothes, towels, or sheets
- Following a recipe
- Making a household budget
- Mopping the floor
- Mowing the lawn
- Organizing a closet, cupboard, shed, attic or garage
- Painting a room
- Plumbing
- Raking leaves
- Setting the table
- Sweeping the floor
- Taking out the trash
- Tracking personal finances
- Vacuuming
- Vegetable gardening
- Wallpapering
- Washing clothes, dishes, windows or the car

❖ Examples of Personal Life Skills

- Caring
- Common sense
- Cooperation
- Curiosity
- Effort
- Flexibility
- Friendship
- Initiative
- Integrity
- Organization
- Patience
- Perseverance
- Problem solving
- Responsibility
- Sense of humour

❖ Personal Skills for Body and Mind

Self-preservation, i.e., staying healthy both mentally and physically, is possibly the most fundamental of all skills. Some ideas of this part will help you stay fit and develop good interpersonal, leadership and presentation skills. One of them has the objective to providing you with practical advice on personal skills in order to boost your mental and physical health and well-being.

Learning about Personal Development

The skills of personal development can kindle your interest to set personal goals and to achieve personal empowerment. Through personal development, they will also help you build a set of strong and effective skills, which will enable you to take relevant and positive decisions and choices later on.

❖ Personal Development Skills

Personal development and empowerment skills develop a framework to set personal goals and achieving them in life.

- Be more self-aware and learn to recognize your strengths and weaknesses, and those of others, that is, develop the habit of reflective practice.
- Learn how to speak impressively with a view to encourage self-empowerment, positive thinking and neuro-linguistic programming, and help others to empower themselves.
- Overcome the barriers to learning and developing yourself by discovering the strong mental setup in you and start developing new skills now.

❖ Character Building Skills

However old-fashioned 'character' and 'virtue' are, yet they are the prominent and most important character-building skills in today's world.

Learn the importance of emotional intelligence, how to manage emotions by gaining mastery over yourself, and develop the ability to understand yourself and others.

Learn how to manage your emotions effectively, use your moral compass, and a framework for learning, as these are the most important ways to live well.

Recognize the importance of ethics as they play a major role in life.

Find out plenty of character traits, and explore the issues of self-control, developing resilience, placid disposition, or even friendliness or compassion. There are many more to discover which will help you feel good about yourself.

Overcome the barriers and learn to accept your own strengths and weaknesses by building confidence and self-esteem as our feelings leave impact on many aspects of our everyday life. Further your understanding of confidence and self-esteem by reading our pages on personal development and presentation, how we dress ourselves and look after our physical appearances.

❖ Assertiveness

It is very important to develop the skills of assertiveness for self-development. Assertiveness does not mean being aggressive or passive, it means to develop an understanding of ourselves and communicate our beliefs, values and opinions with others. Find out more about assertiveness—why people are not assertive and dealing with non-assertiveness and assertiveness techniques.

❖ Time Management and Its Positive Effect on Life

Our time management techniques have a direct effect on our life. This hints at some of the ways to improve your effectiveness at getting things done, so that you can achieve more and feel more motivated and self-confident. Often there are lot of things that distract us and waste our time from doing the important works, so, to avoid wasting time and reduce these distractions and achieve the goals, we must prioritize, categorize and organize our time.

❖ Stress and Stress Management

Stress, nowadays, is common in our life. We always feel the need of balancing family, health, work, money and so on. Stress makes us seriously ill. Therefore, we have some valuable suggestions on how to manage, reduce and avoid stress in life. We hope these will help you find the ways to get rid of stress.

- **Recognizing Stress:** Recognizing the signs of stress could be helpful in learning more about its causes, and the way it may reveal itself in behaviour.
- **Avoiding Stress:** By finding the reasons behind stress and stress causing agents, stressful situations can be potentially avoided or minimized. Some ways of avoiding stress and tips on relaxation can be discovered thereby.
- **Stress, Nutrition and Diet:** The relationship between diet and its effect on our thinking should be understood. Improvement in diet could lead to better thought process, gain in confidence, better feeling to enjoy life and reduce stress.
- **Stress Associated with the Workplace:** The common factor responsible for many lost working days is workplace stress. An organization need to adopt the following approaches to effectively deal with the stress level of its employees at workplace—finding the reason behind people getting stressed

at work, taking the steps required to alleviate the problem and looking for the ways in which the employer can minimize workplace stress.

- **Tips for Dealing with Stress:** Finding out practical and simple ways to deal with and help combat stress in life is required.
- **Relaxation Techniques:** Simple and effective ways to relax should be discovered.
- **Work-life Balance:** The way to maintain a healthy balance between work and leisure time should be discovered.

❖ Anger, Anger Management and Aggression

As defined, Anger is 'the strong feeling that you have when something has happened that you think is bad and unfair'. Anger is a natural emotion and everyone get angry from time to time. The root causes of anger are stress, frustration, feelings of wrong doing. The way of handling and managing this emotion is different for every human. Herein we will learn about anger and how to manage it, especially about:

❖ What is anger?

Anger management and anger management therapy: What to expect?

In many countries, aggressive behaviour towards others is intolerable and a criminal offence. Aggression can be very destructive both mentally and physically for all involved.

Interpersonal Skills

The life skills that someone uses to share their thoughts and interact with other people, individually and in group, are called interpersonal skills. People who have strong command on interpersonal skills are generally more successful in both their professional and personal lives and employers often hire staffs with 'strong interpersonal skills' as they require those people who work effectively in a team and able to communicate effectively with colleagues, customers and clients.

The value of interpersonal skills is not just limited to workplace only, our personal and social lives can also benefit from better interpersonal skills. A person with effective interpersonal skills is perceived as optimistic, calm, confident, etc. For improving interpersonal skills, you can interact with others and you will need to put in a lot of efforts for attaining this skill.

❖ Interpersonal Skills' Self-Assessment

Discover your interpersonal skills: Listening skills, verbal communication, emotional intelligence and teamwork are included in interpersonal skills.

❖ Interpersonal skills are listed as follows

- **Verbal Communication:** It is about what we say and the way to say it.
- **Non-Verbal Communication:** It is about communicating without making use of words; body language is an example of non-verbal communication.
- **Listening Skills:** It is the ability to interpret both the verbal and non-verbal messages sent by others.
- **Negotiation:** It is the way of working with others to arrive at a mutually agreeable (Win/Win) outcome.
- **Problem Solving:** It is the way of working with others to identify, define and solve problems.
- **Decision Making:** It is the way of exploring and analysing options to make sound decisions.
- **Assertiveness:** It is about communicating our values, ideas, beliefs, opinions, needs and wants freely.

Develop your interpersonal skills: To develop interpersonal skills, learn about methods of improving your communication skills, tackle conflict resolution, mediate in difficult situations, and develop your emotional intelligence. Interpersonal skills are used in everyday life. People need little time and effort to develop these skills and the fact is that good interpersonal skills can improve many aspects of your life, professionally and socially, and they lead to better understanding and better relationships. Sometimes, interpersonal skills are also referred as social skills, people skills, soft skills, communication skills or life skills. However, strong interpersonal skill is the base of many other skills, since these are important to our personal relationships, social affairs and professional lives. It is very difficult to develop other important life skills in the absence of interpersonal skills.

Here are some ways to improve and develop your interpersonal skills:

- ***Learn to listen***: Listening is different from hearing. Listening is the process of interpreting whatever you hear from the speaker. Listening is one of the characteristics of effective interpersonal skills. Listener should concentrate on the speaker for their verbal and non-verbal communication. To learn more about listening skills, you can visit websites related to communication skills.
- ***Choose your words***: While talking to others, be aware of the words you are using with another person. There are chances that you could be misunderstood or your words may be misinterpreted; so, in this kind of scenario, you should practice clarity and learn to seek feedback to ensure your message has been understood properly. Try to learn more and more about verbal communication, effective speech and how to use your voice; in addition, encourage others to engage in communication and use meaningful questionnaire to develop your understanding.
- ***Understand why communication fails***: There are many reasons behind the failure of communication. To overcome from the barriers such as ineffective interpersonal communication and misunderstanding, learn and analyse about the barriers and start working on these barriers one by one and improve yourself.
- ***Relax***: Many times, while we become nervous, we start talking faster and less clearly. In this situation, it is very important to control our nervousness. So, instead of getting nervous, try to stay calm, keep patience, make eye contact, smile and be confident. Try to adopt various relaxation techniques and take time to relax.
- ***Clarify***: For an effective communication, try to be interactive and show interest in the people you talk with. For the statements that can be easily misunderstood, ask questions and go for clarification.

- ***Be positive***: Remove all the negativity and remain positive and cheerful. If you maintain a positive attitude, then people will get attracted towards you and will show interest while talking to you.
- ***Empathize***: As people may have different points of view so try to understand their views and respect their views. Try to understand from their viewpoint. While gaining the respect and trust of others, you will learn many things.
- ***Understand stress***: Stress may have positive as well as negative impacts. Working under pressure is a good quality and every employer looks for the same person. So, one should learn to recognize, manage and reduce stress.
- ***Learn to be assertive:*** Assertiveness is a good quality and an individual should be neither passive nor aggressive. Assertiveness is about expressing your feelings and opinions with confidence so that others can understand and respect your views.
- ***Reflect and improve***: Learn from your previously done mistakes during conversations and other personal interactions and improve yourself. Keeping a positive attitude is good but always remember that you can improve your soft skills at any point of time.
- ***Negotiate***: Effective negotiation is a quality and it is important to learn about effective negotiation with others paving the way to mutual respect, trust and long-term social relations.
- ***Working in groups***: A candidate must learn about different types of groups and teams, and learn how to work in team. Working in groups is a skill and every employer is in search of such candidates, in fact in many situations, we have to deal with groups, professionally and socially.

Leadership Skills and Leadership Styles

Often people become leaders because they have trustworthiness and people want to follow them. Leadership is a very responsible job as a large number of people depend on you and follow your advices. To lead a team or group, there is a requirement of number of key skills. Leadership roles are not limited to working environment only but it can be applied to any situation such as to lead a group, professionally, socially and at home. While dealing with people in such a way as to motivate, enthuse and build respect, leadership skills are sought after by employers.

The two questions which are generally asked about leadership:

What exactly is a leader?

How is being a leader different from being a manager?

Leadership is a skill that cannot be taught. Many people think that leadership can be taught. Many academicians and those offering leadership training or literature of some sort are convinced that they can provide leadership skill training to the people but according to some successful leaders, leadership is the state of mind. They had never taken any formal training and it is their trait that makes them successful leaders.

The way of leadership for all leaders is not similar. A famous joke we all have heard about 'mushroom' leadership (keep them in the dark and feed them on manure) and 'seagulls' (swoop in, squawk, and drop unpleasant things on people). Apart from jokes, there are many different styles of leadership and different leadership styles are suitable for different people and different circumstances, but the best leader is one who learns to use them all.

You can improve your leadership skills by learning about it and practicing more and more. Implementation of leadership skill is different and requires different set of skills and attitudes. 'Can leadership be taught?' This question has no simple answer and it is not possible to argue on this topic. So, keep an open mind on the topic and gather information about the skills required by a good leader.

❖ Skills Required by Good Leaders

Here are some skills mentioned below to be a good leader:

An important skill a leader requires is the ability to think strategically. Leaders have a vision of where they want to be and work to achieve that vision.

Strategic thinking develops organizing and action planning and both are essential for the achievement of your vision and strategy. The risk management skills help you avoid things going wrong, and manage if this kind of issue occurs.

Leaders should have the ability to make decision in line with the strategy to be executed.

During leadership, a leader may face many problems and solving these problems effectively is another leadership skill. A leader sees a problem as an opportunity and through their experiences and try to solve it.

Leaders should be organized on a personal level, and have the ability to manage themselves and their time properly.

Leaders have to spend a bit of time on themselves, especially on their self-motivation along with organizing their time and their teams. If a leader lacks the quality of self-motivation, then he will struggle to motivate others.

❖ Developing People Skills

The skills required for leading team members is another area that is crucial for leaders. The reality is without followers, there are no leaders. To deal with people on a one-to-one and group basis, leaders should be able to work with group and to deal with different situations. One of the skills that new leaders need to learn is how to delegate. Delegation can give team members responsibility and help them to remain motivated. Leaders should have qualities to give their views on personal performance to others in a way that will be positive rather than destructive, and leaders should have the patience to hear others' opinions of them. Another tool required by the leaders is to understand the way that others behave, and start positive interactions. At last, leaders should be able to work properly in group.

❖ Effective Personal Qualities

The leaders tend to display a number of personality traits that differentiates them from the rest. Though these qualities are intrinsic, but these can also be developed and improved over time.

The leadership qualities in a person include: charisma, a quality of 'brightness', which draws the people to follow him; assertiveness, the quality which enables that person to put forth their point of view without aggression, but firmly; and empathy, which is an understanding of other's feelings.

Leadership qualities could be understood in terms of emotional intelligence, which is measured in terms of the ability to relate well with others and to a person's own feelings.

❖ Excellent Communication

Excellent communication skills are one of the essential requirements for becoming a leader. Successful leaders need to show high level of skills during communicating with others, as they have to deal with various kinds of persons. Good leaders need to be extremely good listeners, able to listen actively and elicit information by relevant questioning. Leaders should have the ability to build relationship quickly and effectively with others, whether peers or subordinates. Usually, they are very well at public speaking, equally skilled at getting their point across in a formal presentation, Board meeting, or in an informal meeting. Along with the above qualities, leaders should have strong negotiation skills, in the widest sense, in terms of reaching win-win situations and making sure that they know their 'bottom line'.

Learning Skills

Learning is also a quality and it is the most crucial skill for personal development. Nowadays, learning skills are called the 4 C's: critical thinking, creative thinking, communicating, and collaborating. These 4 C's are important to succeed in school and for pursuing higher studies also.

❖ Critical Thinking

Critical thinking is one of the 4 C's and defined as focused, careful analysis of something to better interpret it. Generally, when people discuss about 'left brain' activity, they refer to critical thinking. Some of the main critical thinking abilities are given below:

❖ Creative Thinking

Creativity means 'being able to come up with something new'. Critical thinking can be defined in many ways. Creative thinking is 'the process of actively and skilfully conceptualizing, applying, analysing, synthesizing, and evaluating information to reach an answer or conclusion'. When people discuss about 'right brain' activity, they usually mean creative thinking. Here are some of the most common creative thinking abilities:

Brainstorming ideas involve questioning and rapidly finding solution, even those that are far-fetched, impractical, or difficult.

Creating something means to form something by combining materials, perhaps in accordance to a plan or based on the instinct of the moment.

Designing something means finding the association between form and function and giving shape to the materials for a specific purpose.

Entertaining others involves telling stories, cracking jokes, singing songs, playing games, playing music, acting out parts and carrying out conversation.

Imagining ideas involves using thinking process to reach into the unknown and impossible, perhaps idly or with great concentration, as done by Einstein through his thought experiments.

Improvising a solution means using something in an innovative way to find a solution to a problem.

Innovating is developing something that was non-existent before, whether an object, a procedure or an idea.

Overturning something means flipping it in order to get a new point of view, perhaps by redefining givens, reversing cause and effect, or considering something in a brand new way.

Problem solving requires making use of many of the creative abilities listed here to find out possible solutions and putting one or more of them into action.

Questioning helps us to know the unknown, to look for information or a novel way to do something.

❖ Communicating

Analysing the situation means thinking the situation in context of the subject, purpose, sender, receiver, medium and message.

Choosing a medium involves to decide upon the most suitable way for delivering a message, ranging from a face-to-face chat to a 400-page report.

Evaluating messages means to find out whether they are complete, correct, reliable, authoritative and up-to-date.

Following conventions refers to communicating using the anticipated norms for the medium chosen.

Listening actively means cautiously paying attention, taking notes, asking questions, and otherwise getting engaged in the ideas being communicated.

Reading means decoding written words and images to understand the meaning communicated by their originator.

Speaking means making use of words uttered from mouth, tone of voice, body language, gestures, facial expressions, and visual aids in order to convey ideas.

Turn taking refers to effective switching from receiving ideas to providing ideas, to and fro between those in the communication situation.

Using technology requires realizing the abilities and limitations associated with any technological communication, from phone calls to e-mails to instant messages.

Writing means to encode messages into words, sentences and paragraphs to communicate to a person who is removed by distance, time, or both.

❖ Collaborating

Allocating resources and responsibilities ensures that all members of a team can work in the most favourable manner.

Brainstorming ideas in a group involves quickly finding and writing down ideas without pausing for their critical review.

Decision-making refers to sorting through the several options provided to the group and reaching out a single option for consideration.

Delegating refers to assigning duties to different members of a group and expecting all of them to fulfil their respective tasks.

Evaluating the products, processes and members of the group gives a clear idea of what is working well and what improvements are required.

Goal setting by the group calls for analysing the situation, decide upon the desired outcome and clearly stating an achievable objective.

Leading a group means creation of a feasible environment in which all members can contribute by making the maximum use of their abilities.

Managing time means to match up a list of tasks to a schedule and keeping track of the progress towards goals.

Resolving conflicts requires using any of the following strategies: asserting, cooperating, competing, compromising, or deferring.

Team building refers to working cooperatively over time towards achievement of a common goal.

Presentation Skills

Presentation is the process of describing any topic to the group of people by speech and audio-visual medium. It can be formal or informal. The main goal of presentation is to give information, to convince the audience to act and to create goodwill. An effective presentation contains good subject matter, should match with the objective, should best fit the audience and should be well organized. The presentation skill is required everywhere which is dependent on confidence.

❖ Characteristics of a Good/Effective Presentation

For the effective presentation, some points are given below:

Before starting the presentation, analyse the needs, age, educational background, language and culture of the target audience. Whatever messages or ideas are to be delivered by the presentation that should be according to the audience interest, and the audience should be well convinced by the presenter.

A good presentation should be brief and focused on the topic.

A good presentation should have the capability to convey the required information.

During presentation, transform your fear into positive energy and be calm and relaxed.

Make an eye contact during the entire presentation and focus on conveying your message well, and use a positive body language.

For effective presentation, the speaker should use more visual aids like diagrams, pictures and charts, etc., as we know humans learn more from visual aids. Each slide should contain limited information only. Organize all the visuals for making a logical and sound presentation.

Try to face the audience rather than the screen, and the speaker should not block the view.

Before starting the presentation, plan and organize the presentation like the beginning of presentation, content of the presentation and ending of the presentation. It is very important to not lose the interest of audience.

To deliver better presentation with confidence, it is required to rehearse and practice your presentation. At the end of presentation, summarize the presentation, encourage the audience to ask more questions and answer those questions honestly.

The appearance of the speaker should be presentable during presentation and use short and simple words.

Add positive quotes, humour or remarkable facts to maintain the audience interest.

The speaker should discuss about the objectives of the presentation at the beginning of the presentation.

Writing Skills

Writing skills that effectively help you to communicate at workplace are an important part of communication. Good writing skills allow you to communicate your message with ease to a larger audience. To write a report, plan or strategize at work, write a grant application or press release within a volunteering role, etc., every area needs effective writing skills. In fact, if you want to get a job, then your CV should be free from grammatical errors. In publishing area, everyone needs effective writing skills. If readers would spot a spelling or grammatical mistake, then readers will have an immediate negative reaction. For example, the customers would doubt credibility of the website and the organization if they find a spelling mistake on a commercial web page.

❖ Grammar, Spelling and Punctuation

The main features of written communication are correct grammar, punctuation and spelling. During writing, it is the responsibility of the writer to check the content for accuracy; otherwise, the reader will form a negative opinion for the writer and content. In the similar way, some employers state that any CV or resume can be rejected in case of spelling and grammatical error. A BBC news article quotes research that spelling mistakes cost online businesses 'millions' in lost sales. Owing to the grammatical mistakes in the content, it takes more time to understand the text as the person who reads have to think and re-read the text to understand it.

❖ Improving Your Writing Skills

There are many ways to improve the writing skills. Writing is a skill that can be improved by learning and practicing it. By reading aloud the content, writing skills can be improved. While reading, it is very important to read the content with concentration. Reading also helps you to expand your vocabulary.

❖ Writing under Specific Circumstances

Many times in life, you have to write about something specific, for example, notes of a conversation, minutes of formal meeting, preparing a report, etc. All these need good writing skills and usually a particular writing style.

❖ Writing in the Workplace

Writing is a skill and it needs regular practice. Writing skill is very important at workplace. The employers look for those candidates who have excellent writing skills and who can write with clarity.

❖ Writing Job Applications

In formal communication, many times we have to write application to the higher authorities; writing skill is also important in writing a job application.

❖ Writing for Study

Along with workplace, writing skill is also a part of course of study, be it college or university.

Numeracy Skills

❖ Numeracy Skills Count

For better paid jobs, greater well-being and a less stressful life, numeracy skills are important. Numeracy skills are not limited to scientists, accountants and the tax man; in fact, many professions need at least a basic level of knowledge in numeracy and mathematics. So, to improve numeracy skills, take some time to develop your numeracy skills. Chris Humphries, Chairman of National Numeracy, talking to the BBC said: "It is simply inexcusable for anyone to say: 'I can't do maths'...".

Numeracy skills are fundamental mathematical skills, and poor numeracy can affect the organization and people a lot. Numeracy skills include the abilities to analyse the numerical calculation and to make the right conclusions; it also includes the ability to express ideas and situations using numerical or mathematical information.

Numeracy is also related to employment, as adults with weak numeracy skills are more unemployed than those who have some skill in numeracy. Adults who have basic knowledge of numeracy skills can earn more than who lack the skills to solve mathematical calculations.

The fact is people with weak numerical skills are less able to save money in comparison to others. In addition, they are less able to negotiate for the best deals on financial products. It has been found in a research that debt problems can be the reason of stress.

❖ Develop Your Numeracy Skills

From the above it is clear that numeracy skills are important everywhere from daily life to working in the organization. Everybody has the ability to learn basic mathematics and knowledge of basic numeracy and mathematics will help you in all aspects of your life, for example, numeracy skills make you more employable, save your time and money and improve your well-being and reduce stress, etc.

Parenting Skills

Good parenting skills could be of great help to children in the development of their overall personality traits to grow into healthy, productive and successful adults. The overall health status of a growing child takes into account both physical and emotional aspects of his health. Couples who are about to become parents may feel discouraged at the prospect of developing the skills required for being successful parents, but parenting skills can also be improved with practice and dedication just like other skills. Parenting skills are the positive traits of a 'good parent' acting as guiding forces to provide right direction to a child to enable him to grow into a healthy adult. Parenting skills play an effective role to influence the development; maintenance and cessation of children's negative and positive behaviours. Good parenting requires a lot of skill and patience and is about putting constant efforts in the right direction. The quality of the parents' interactions with their children during the early years of their growth is a crucial factor in developing of their cognitive potential, social skills and behavioural functioning.

It benefits the children (avoids poor developmental outcomes) most when their parents adopt the following parenting methods:

Truthful communication with the children about events or discussions that have happened, and when parents explain clearly to children the incident that happened and the way they were found involved if they were;

Parents need to adopt consistent behaviour or routine, as children need structure. Parents who set regular routines for children to follow, provide benefits to their behavioural pattern;

Make maximum utilization of the available resources, reaching out to the community;

Parents need to show more interest in their child's educational and early development needs; and

They should adopt open communication with their children and be informed about the surroundings of their child, his activities related to learning and doing things and the overall effect of all these things on the child.

It is often assumed that parenting skills are self-evident or naturally present in parents. However, those coming from a negative/vulnerable environment might have a tendency to pass on their suffering to their families or for those having incorrect beliefs or poorer understanding of developmental milestones engage with their children in only the way they know which may lead to problematic parenting resulting in adverse effects on the children. Parenting practices are particularly risk prone during marital transitions such as divorce, separation and remarriage. In case of children failing to adjust to these adverse circumstances, there could be risk of negative outcomes.

❑❑❑

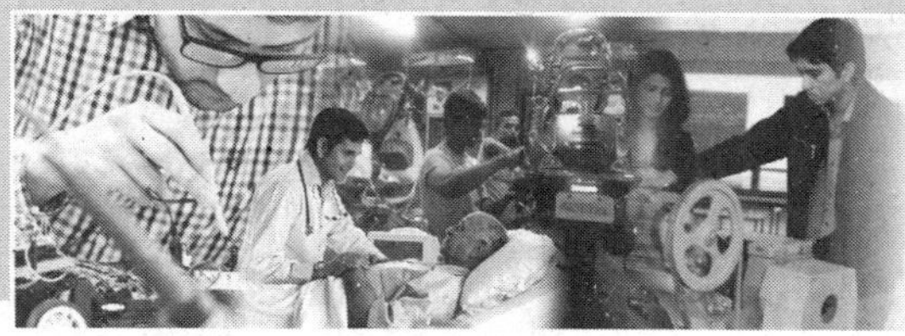

Chapter 4

Indian Economy: Present Challenges and Future Outlook

India is home to 1.34 billion people—18% of the world's population. It will have overtaken China as the world's most populous country by 2024. It has the world's largest youth population, but isn't yet fully capturing this potential demographic dividend—over 30% of India's youth are NEETs (not in employment, education or training), according to the OECD.

Indian Economy—2018: Prospects and Challenges

India is poised to win back its tag of the fastest growing economy in the world. The recent upgrade of India's rating by the US based credit rating agency Moody's (Baa2 from Baa3) in recognition of the reforms agenda pursued by the Government is a major boost to investor confidence. Further, as the short term disruptions caused by major reforms such as the Goods and Services Tax (GST) and demonetization recede, the economy is on the rebound and is likely to achieve higher growth targets in the New Year.

❖ Macroeconomic Performances

GDP Growth

Gross Domestic Product (GDP) is on a recovery path after slowdown in the first quarter of 2017–18, and real GDP growth for the second quarter (2QFY18) increased to 6.3% from 5.7% in the previous quarter, a likely fallout of the introduction of GST. The second half of 2017–18 will witness a higher growth rate, and this is further expected to consolidate in the coming New Year, as the benefits of GST and other reforms gain traction.

Sectoral Growth

The agricultural sector registered moderate growth as erratic monsoon in several parts and flooding in some states impacted performance.

Industrial growth accelerated sharply during the second quarter of FY 2018 and jumped to 6.9% from 1.5% in the previous quarter, on account of a sharp increase in manufacturing and electricity, gas, water supply and utility services. Manufacturing registered an impressive growth at 7% in 2QFY18 as compared to 1.2% posted in the first quarter.

Services sector grew only marginally at 6.6% in the second quarter as compared to 7.8% in the previous quarter.

Inflation

The economy saw high inflation during October 2017 owing to elevated food prices. Going forward, this is likely to be contained on account of a good harvest and favorable monsoons.

The impact of GST on prices is likely to become clearer in the coming year as the teething problems related to its implementation ease out. Further, the GST Council's decision to cut tax rates on 177 items is also expected to partially ease the inflationary pressure, as the companies start passing the benefits of lower prices to consumers.

External Sector

Healthy foreign fund inflows caused the rupee to strengthen during the latter half of the year. The recent Moody's upgrade is likely to encourage further inflows and the rupee could appreciate further. On the other hand, the impact of the decision in the US to raise interest rates and introduce tax cuts may work the other way. In any case, India's consumer markets are expected to remain a strong incentive to FDI.

A contraction in export growth pushed the merchandise trade deficit to a near 3-year high in October 2017, which was forcefully reversed in November with a positive growth rate of over 30%. With the streamlining of GST related issues and some changes in GST rules by the Government as well as firming of global recovery, export growth will emerge as a powerful growth driver in 2018.

Monetary Policy

The Reserve Bank of India (RBI) kept policy rates unchanged in its fifth bi-monthly monetary policy meeting on 6th December, 2017. However, industry is hopeful that going forward, RBI would lower interest rates to boost broad-based investment and consumption activity which in turn would promote economic growth.

Credit Growth

Credit growth to the non-food sector shows encouraging signs of pick-up in the last few months. Recapitalization of Public Sector Banks may bolster credit flows further and ease their stressed assets situation.

CII Business Confidence Index

The Business Confidence Index (BCI) by Confederation of Indian Industry (CII), climbed up to 59.7 during October-December 2017 as against 58.3 in the previous quarter. This increase was a result of improvement in the perception regarding overall economic conditions and expectations of improved business situation post the recent disruptions which prompted companies to be optimistic about favourable economic growth in the future. The findings are part of CII's 101st edition of quarterly Business Outlook Survey, based on around 200 responses from large, medium, small and micro firms, covering all regions of the country.

The recovery recorded in the index coupled with India's sharp improvement in the Ease of Doing Business rankings (India jumped 30 places to 100) this year reinforces company perception that demands pick up is underway. Most of the respondents in the survey also believe that GST payments would become hassle-free by Q1 2018-19.

❖ Challenges

Firms rated low domestic demand followed by high commodity prices as main concerns in CII's Business Outlook Survey. Stepping up private investment remains a major macroeconomic challenge in the next year.

Inflationary pressures also remain a concern. Though food prices are likely to be contained on account of favorable monsoons, caution must be exercised as upside risks still remain in the form of implementation of farm loan waiver and 7th Pay Commission hand-outs.

India's share in world exports is currently at 1.8%. Efforts to increase this figure by way of providing export credit to manufacturers, increasing the capital base of Export Credit Guarantee Scheme of the Export Credit Guarantee Corporation (ECGC), increasing subvention to 4% etc. must be undertaken.

The economy benefitted from increased foreign inflows during the latter half of 2017. While this is good news, efforts to contain further appreciation of the rupee should be in place as further strengthening may affect exports and job creation.

Bank credit growth hit a 20 year low in 2016–17 with Non-Performing Assets (NPAs) at 9.9%. India has been ranked fifth on the list of countries with highest NPAs. Though bank recapitalization efforts are underway, the economy needs to recover from the bad loan problem quickly for favourable economic growth in the future.

The infrastructure deficit is a major concern and infrastructure investment needs to be stepped up as currently it is not in par with the needs of the economy.

Other challenges for the economy include addressing infrastructural bottlenecks in the agricultural sector, investment in human resources to leverage the demographic dividend, increasing expenditure on education and healthcare sectors, and social security provision for the unorganized sector.

With on-going reforms that are beginning to positively impact the economy, CII is optimistic about Indian growth prospects in

2018. At the same time, policymakers need to be watchful and address the current macroeconomic challenges for a sustainable and fruitful recovery.

Transformation of Indian Economy

Twenty-five years ago, India embarked on a journey of economic liberalization, opening its doors to globalization and market forces. We, and the rest of the world, have watched as the investment and trade regime introduced in 1991 raised economic growth, increased consumer choice, and reduced poverty significantly.

Now, as uncertainties cloud the global economic picture, the International Monetary Fund has projected that India's GDP will grow by 7.4 percent for 2016–17, making it the world's fastest-growing large economy. India also compares favorably with other emerging markets in growth potential. The country offers an attractive long-term future powered largely by a consuming class that's expected to more than triple, to 89 million households, by 2025.

Liberalization has created new opportunities. The challenge for policy makers is to manage growth so that it creates the basis for sustainable economic performance. Although much work has been done, India's transformation into a global economic force has yet to fully benefit all its citizens. There's a massive unmet need for basic services, such as water and sanitation, energy, and health care, for example, while red tape makes it hard to do business. The government has begun to address many of these challenges, and the pace of change could accelerate in coming years as some initiatives gain scale.

❖ From Poverty to Empowerment: Acceptable Living Standards for all

The trickle-down effect of economic liberalization has lifted millions of Indians from indigence in the past two decades. The official poverty rate declined from 45 percent of the population in 1994 to 22 percent in 2012, but this statistic defines only the most dismal situations. By our broader measure of minimum acceptable living standards—spanning nutrition, water, sanitation, energy, housing, education, and healthcare—we find that 56 percent of Indians lacked the basics in 2012.

The country will need to address these gaps to achieve its potential. The task is certainly within India's capacity, but policy makers will have to promote an agenda emphasizing job creation, growth-oriented investment, farm-sector productivity, and innovative social programs that help the people who actually need them. The private sector has a substantial role to play both in creating and providing effective basic services.

❖ Sustainable Urbanization: Building India's Growth Engines

By 2025, MGI estimates, India will have 69 cities with a population of more than one million each. Economic growth will center on them, and the biggest infrastructure building will take place there. The output of Indian cities will come to resemble that of cities in middle-income nations. In 2030, for example, Mumbai's economy, a mammoth market of $245 billion in consumption, will be bigger than Malaysia's today. The next four cities by market size will each have annual consumption of $80 billion to $175 billion by 2030.

To achieve sustainable growth, these cities will have to become more livable places, offering clean air and water, reliable utilities, and extensive green spaces. India's urban transformation represents a huge opportunity for domestic and international businesses that can provide capital, technology, and planning know-how, as well as the goods and services urban consumers demand.

❖ Manufacturing for India, in India

Although India's manufacturing sector has lagged behind China's, there will be substantial opportunities to invest in value-creating businesses and to create jobs. India's appeal to potential investors will be more than just its low-cost labor: manufacturers there are building competitive businesses to tap into the large and growing local market. Further reforms and public infrastructure investments could make it easier for all types of manufacturing businesses—foreign and Indian alike—to achieve scale and efficiency.

❖ Riding the Digital Wave: Harnessing Technology for India's Growth

Twelve powerful technologies will benefit India, helping to raise productivity, improving efficiency across major sectors of the economy, and radically altering the provision of services such as education and healthcare. These technologies could add $550 billion to $1 trillion a year of economic value in 2025, according to our analysis, potentially creating millions of well-paying, productive jobs (including positions for people with moderate levels of formal education) and helping millions of Indians to enjoy a decent standard of living.

❖ Unlocking the Potential of Indian Women

The research suggests that women now contribute only 17 percent of India's GDP and make up just 24 percent of the workforce, compared with 40 percent globally. In the coming decade, they will represent one of the largest potential economic forces in the country. If it matched the progress toward gender parity of the region's fastest-improving country, we estimate that it could add $700 billion to its GDP in 2025. Movement toward closing the gender gap in education and in financial and digital inclusion has begun, but there is scope for further progress.

Conclusion

It has been stated that India would be able to keep its rate of annual GDP growth not below than 8% up to 2020 and within coming fifty years surpass the Economy of China. India would also gradually deregulate its labour market policy with the passage of time and bring about remarkable change in the field of education and training. Policy of more reform oriented programmes would be taken up and participation of multinational companies through merger and acquisitions would take place rapidly in the foreseeable future resulting in more economic activities. India is thus poised to take a definite turn in view of its micro as well as macroeconomic front.

References: PIB, The Indian Express, The Hindu

❑❑❑

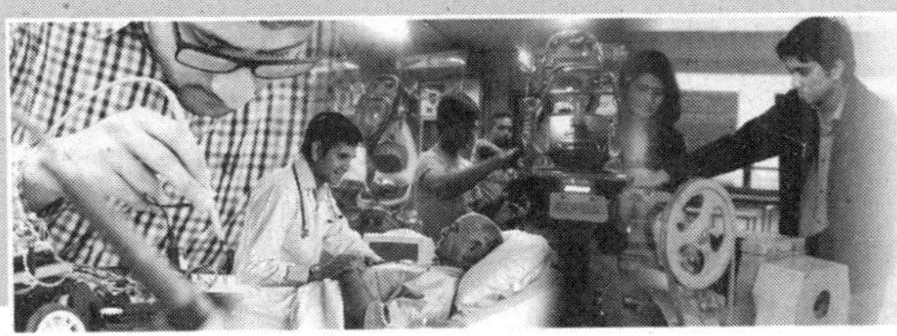

Chapter 5

The Role of Micro and Small Industries for Promotion of Employment Generation in India

The MSMEs are credited with generating the highest rates of employment growth and account for a major share of industrial production and exports. As far as India's growth opportunity is concerned, MSME can be the backbone for the existing and future high growth business.

The Indian MSME sector provides maximum opportunities for both self-employment and wage-employment outside the agricultural sector and contributes in building an inclusive and sustainable society in innumerable ways through creation of non-farm livelihood at low cost, balanced regional development, gender and social balance, environmentally sustainable development, etc.

The MSME sector in India continues to demonstrate remarkable resilience in the face of trialing global and domestic economic circumstances. The sector has sustained an annual growth rate of over 10% for the past few years. With its agility and dynamism, the sector has shown admirable innovativeness and adaptability to survive economic shocks, even of the gravest nature.

The small-scale industries sector plays a vital role in the growth of the country. It contributes almost 40% of the gross industrial value added in the Indian economy. It has been estimated that a million rupees of investment in fixed assets in the small scale sector produces 4.62 million worth of goods or services with an approximate value addition of ten percentage points.

When the performance of this sector is viewed against growth in the manufacturing and the industry sector as a whole, it instills confidence in the resilience of the small-scale sector.

SSI Sector in India creates largest employment opportunities for the Indian populace, next only to Agriculture. It has been estimated that 100,000 rupees of investment in fixed assets in the small-scale sector generates employment for four persons.

Role of MSMEs

- The significance of MSMEs is attributable to their caliber for employment generation, low capital and technology requirement.
- According to the estimates of the Ministry of MSME, Government of India, the sector generates around 100 million jobs through over 46 million units situated throughout the geographical expanse of the country.
- As per the Report of the Working Group on Micro, Small and Medium Enterprises (MSMEs) Growth for 12th Five Year Plan (2012-2017), the sector accounts for 45 % of the manufacturing output and 40 % of total exports of the country.
- The labour to capital ratio in MSMEs and the overall growth in the sector is much higher than that in the large industries. The geographic distribution of the MSMEs is also more even. Thus, MSMEs are important for meeting the national objectives of growth with equity and inclusion.
- They are also important for promotion of industrial development in rural areas, use of traditional or inherited skill, use of local resources, mobilization of resources and exportability of products.

- Besides the wide range of services provided by the sector, the sector is engaged in the manufacturing of over 6,000 products ranging from traditional to hi-tech items.

Case Study – Handloom sector in Kerala

The handloom sector in Kerala employs about 1.75 lakh of people directly and indirectly and this stands second to the coir sector in providing employment among the traditional industries of the state. The handloom industry in the state is concentrated in Thiruvananthapuram, Kannur, Kozhikode, Palakkad, Ernakulam, Thrissur, Kollam and Kasargode Districts. The Kerala Kasavu sarees are praised by women all over India for their fineness of count and natural colours, texture and golden borders. Kerala is also known for the manufacture of cotton handloom fabrics in Kannur, Vadagara and Kozhikode and has captured an export market. Balaramapuram in Thiruvananthapuram district is the most historically important and one of the oldest handloom centers in Kerala. The weavers belonging to Chaliyas community migrated from Nagarcoil and Thirunelveli in Tamil Nadu during the period of Balaramavarma, ruler of Travancore about 250 years back. Kuthampully in Thrissur District is also well known for handloom fabrics. In Kuthampully Devangas migrated from Karnataka are engaged in weaving. It is believed that this community of traditional weavers was brought by the Kochi Royal family about 500 years ago.

Major Initiatives by the Government

- Government's policy initiatives like enactment of the Micro Small and Medium Enterprises Development (MSMED) Act, 2006;
- Pruning of reserved Small Scale Industries (SSI) list; advising Financial Institutions to increase their flow of credit to the SME sector
- Reservation of items for exclusive manufacture in MSME sector statutorily provided for in the Industries (Development and Regulation) Act, 1951

- The President, under Notification dated May 9, 2007, has amended the Government of India (Allocation of Business) Rules, 1961.
- Pursuant to this amendment, Ministry of Agro and Rural Industries and Ministry of Small Scale Industries were merged into a single Ministry, namely, "Ministry of Micro, Small and Medium Enterprises".

Major Schemes of the Government

❖ Scheme of Fund for Regeneration of Traditional Industries (SFURTI)

The objectives of the scheme are to organize the traditional industries and artisans into clusters to make them competitive and provide support for:

- Their long term sustainability & sustained employment,
- To enhance marketability of products of such clusters,
- To equip traditional artisans of the associated clusters with the improved skills,
- To make provision for common facilities and improved tools and equipments for artisans,
- To strengthen the cluster governance systems with the active participation of the stakeholders,
- To build up innovated and traditional skills, improved technologies, advanced processes, market intelligence and new models of public-private partnerships

❖ Stand-up India Scheme

To facilitate bank loans between ₹ 10 lakh to ₹ 100 lakh to at least one Scheduled Caste (SC) or Scheduled Tribe (ST) borrower and at least one Woman borrower per bank branch of all scheduled commercial banks for setting up a green field enterprise.

The Stand-Up India scheme is based on recognition of the challenges faced by SC, ST and women entrepreneurs in setting up enterprises, obtaining loans and other support needed from time to time for succeeding in business.

❖ Scheme for the Development and Promotion of Women Entrepreneurs

With a view to encourage women in setting up their own ventures, the government implemented a scheme, namely, "Trade Related Entrepreneurship Assistance and Development (TREAD)".

The scheme envisages economic empowerment of women through the development of their entrepreneurial skills in non-farm activities. There are three major components of the scheme:

1. Government of India would grant up to 30% of the total project cost to the NGOs for promoting entrepreneurship among women. The remaining 70% of the project cost is financed by the lending agency as loan for undertaking activities as envisaged in the project.
2. Government of India would grant up to ₹ 1 lakh per programme to training institutions/ NGOs for imparting training to the women entrepreneurs, subject to these institutions/NGOs bring their share to the extent of minimum 25 % of Government of India grant and 10 % in case of NER.
3. Need-based Government of India grants up to ₹ 5 lakh to National Entrepreneurship Development.

Challenges Faced by This Sector

- The sector is always fund starved. Banks are often unwilling to lend. Besides, whatever bank finance these sector gets, comes at far higher interest cost than what large enterprises can negotiate.
- Long receivables cycles make a mess of working capital management.
- Little access to trained labour, technical progress and management support limit their growth.
- Other common problems faced by small enterprises are related to availability of technology, infrastructure and managerial competence, and limitations posed by labour laws, taxation policy, market uncertainty and imperfect competition.

❖ Suggestions

- The challenge now is to create a policy environment that will encourage the growth of more MSME that can hold their own in a competitive market.
- The problems faced by MSMEs need to be considered in a disaggregated manner for successful policy implementation as they produce very diverse products, use different inputs and operate in distinct environments.
- In general, there is need for tax provisions and laws that are not only labour-friendly but also entrepreneur-friendly.
- More importantly, there is need for skill formation and continuous upgrade both for labour and entrepreneurs.
- While the government has to strengthen the existing skilling efforts for labour, there is an urgent need for managerial skill development for entrepreneurs running MSMEs—an area that is considerably neglected.
- Further, the government could consider dedicated television and radio programmes, similar to agriculture, to help educate entrepreneurs running small businesses.

Conclusion

For enabling future growth in Indian economy and increasing GDP, the share of MSME contribution would increase from current 8% to 15% by the year 2020. This would be realized by the growth of the new wave MSME led by entrepreneurship focused on innovation and technologies, creating opportunities for women entrepreneurs, and developing skilled resources.

Issues related to credit, like adequacy, timely availability, cost and mortgages continue to be a concern for MSME. These enterprises are dependent on self-finance. Profit margins are also low. The government drive for financial inclusion could benefit such entities. The government could consider dedicating specialized financial schemes for addressing difficulties in assessing and providing credit for small enterprises, as also providing line of credit to firms which are under financial stress. However, it remains to be seen whether new institutions such as MUDRA Bank can open the credit markets for small enterprises.

❑❑❑

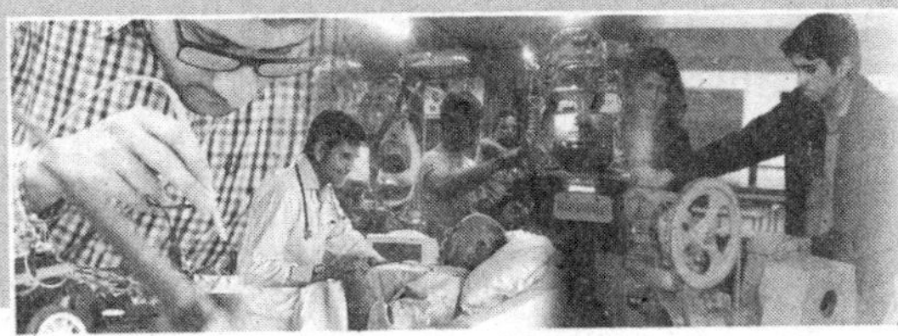

Chapter
6

Role of 'Start Up' and 'Stand Up' in Employment and Self-Employment in NEW INDIA

In quest for expansion, our economy has acquired the dubious distinction of having high unemployment numbers, despite being one of the fastest growing countries in the world. One of the major challenges for India is to provide employment to a growing number of literate and aspiring youths. More than one million youths are joining the country's already bulging pool of unemployed workforce every month.

During the initial plan periods, India pursued the trickle down strategy for mainstreaming millions of underprivileged, but didn't achieve much success. This disappointing experience called for a more direct, inclusive and participatory growth model with greater orientation towards employment generation.

Failure to provide employment may aggravate unrest among the youth, denying the nation the benefits of demographic dividends. Time frame available to address this issue is shrinking fast and we may lose this opportunity forever. Hence, for stable, sustainable and equitable growth, the speed of providing solution assumes significance. All these demand an urgent job-centric economic growth model with its focused and direct interventionist approach to the targeted segments of *aam aadmi*.

The government's schemes like "Stand Up" India and Start Up India are designed as umbrella initiatives aimed to steer a series of other initiatives already undertaken, like Make in India, Digital India, Skilling India, MUDRA, among others. These have potential to trigger an economic revolution.

Understanding "Start Up" and "Stand Up" India Campaigns

Start Ups and entrepreneurship are critical to India's efforts to restart private investment into the economy, in the face of risk aversion, stalled or slow investments from corporate India. 'Start Up India' initiative was launched in January 2016 by Prime Minister Narendra Modi in a move to help Start Ups and catalyze entrepreneurship.

The Start Up India Action Plan lists out a comprehensive set of structural and regulatory reforms—Income tax exemption, easing compliance through reduction of regulations and having fixed qualifications as to what a 'Start Up' is.

The action plan also provided an 80% waiver on patent filing fees by Start Ups and advisory services. It also created a ₹ 10,000 crore fund-of-funds which is to be managed by professionals drawn from the private sector.

The "Stand Up" India initiative is aimed at promoting entrepreneurship among the downtrodden sections of society such as Dalits and women, by providing local employment, through appropriate hand holding backed by concessional funding from banks. Start Up India on the other hand is targeted at promoting innovative ideas to bring solutions in the areas of affordable healthcare, education, social infrastructure etc with the use of technology as a driver and enabler.

Stand Up India is, thus, envisaged to impart direct and focused interventions guided towards segments like SCs/STs and women to bring them in the mainstream of the economy. This will catalyze their entrepreneurial potential to stimulate bottom-up growth. Similarly, Start Up India is aimed at exhorting new generation aspirational youths, who largely belong to the aam aadmi fold and also have greater risk appetite to jump and pursue high-risk-high-return structured entrepreneurial business models.

Eligibility Criteria for A Start-Up Unit

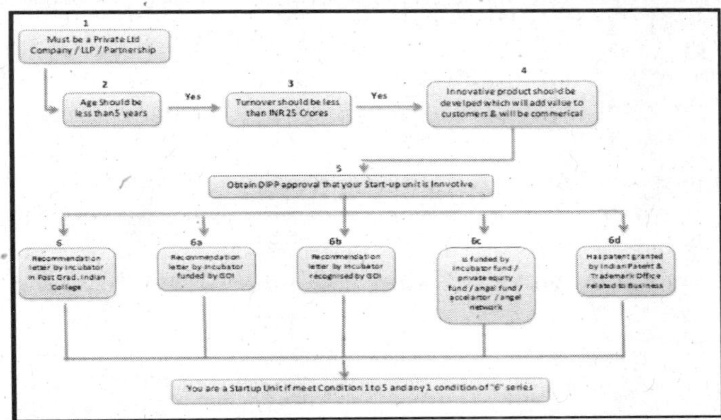

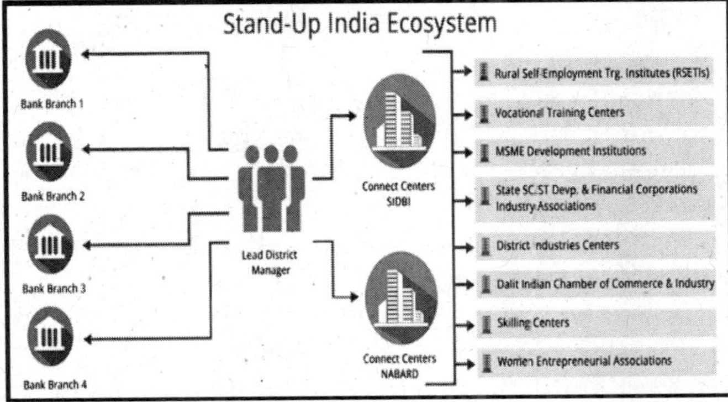

Policies and Action Plans

Start Up India Portal and Mobile App: These have been launched as online platform for providing updates, information, recognition and eligibility certificates to Start Ups and other stakeholders.

Start Up India Hub: Start Up India Hub was operationalised on 1st April 2016 to resolve queries and provide handholding support to Start Ups. The hub has been able to resolve 12,290 queries received from Start Ups through telephone, email and Twitter. To seek clarifications pertaining to Certificate of Recognition as a "Start Up", Certificate of Eligibility to avail tax benefits, seeking information on incubators or funding, one can get in touch with the Hub on Toll-Free number: **1800115565** or email: id **dipp-Startups@nic.in**. Dedicated professionals are handling over 200 queries per day. DIPP has requested State governments and administration of Union Territories to set up hub as well as incubators to help Start Ups during various stages of their life cycle.

Fund of Funds: A 'fund of funds' of INR 10,000 crores to support innovation driven Start Ups has been established which shall be managed by SIDBI. The fund will invest in SEBI registered Alternative Investment Funds (AIFs) which, in turn, will invest in Start Ups. It will act as an enabler to attract private capital in the form of equity, quasi-equity, soft loans and other risk capital for Start Ups. ₹ 500 crore has been released to SIDBI in FY2015-16 and ₹ 600 crore in FY2016-17. First meeting of Venture Capital Investment Committee (VCIC) was held on 12th July, 2016, wherein 13 proposals were examined for funding under FFS and 8 were recommended.

Tax Incentives: The Finance Act, 2016 Section 80- IAC has provision for Start Ups (Companies and LLPs) to get income tax exemption for 3 years in a block of 5 years, if they are incorporated between 1st April 2016 and 31st March 2019. To avail these benefits a Start Up must get a Certificate of Eligibility from the Inter-Ministerial Board.

Tax exemption on investments above Fair Market Value had been introduced on 14 June 2016 for investments made in Start Ups.

Self-Certification: CPCB has exempted industries in "white" category from all the applicable self-certifications under the 3 environment related Acts (The water (Prevention & Control of Pollution) Act, 1974; The Water (Prevention & Control of Pollution) Cess (Amendment) Act, 2003 and The Air (Prevention & Control of Pollution) Act, 1981) listed in the Start Up India Action Plan.

Atal Innovation Mission (AIM): The guidelines for harnessing private sector expertise to set up incubators, organizing annual grand challenge for innovative solutions to problems faced by industry and those posed by ministries as well as a grand challenge for incubators and establishment of tinkering labs have been formulated and published on NITI Aayog's and Start Up India websites.

Relaxed Norms for Public Procurement: Relaxed norms for public procurement for micro and small enterprises have been provisioned in the Procurement Policy of Ministry of MSME.

IPR Benefits: A panel of facilitators has been constituted for assistance in filing Intellectual Property (IP) applications. DIPP would bear the facilitation cost on behalf of Start Ups and also provide rebate in the statutory fee for filing application. To avail IPR-related benefits (rebate in fee and free of cost facilitation in filing IPR applications), a Start Up is required to obtain a Certificate of Recognition from DIPP. Guidelines of the Scheme for Facilitating Start-ups Intellectual Property Protection (SIPP) have been published. Facilitators shall provide assistance to Start Ups in filing and disposal of IP applications related to patents, trademarks and design under relevant Acts. Fast track mechanisms of Start Ups patent applications has been enabled to allow Start Ups to realise the value of their IPRs at the earliest. Further, to enable Start Ups to reduce costs in their crucial formative years, Start Ups shall be provided a rebate of 80% in filing patents (Patent Amendment Rules 2016, May 2016).

Many of these Start Ups are focused to address the societal problems through innovative solutions, be it drinking water, sanitation or rural healthcare among others. Competitive market funding of these "Start Ups" are driven largely by the leverage, outreach and the likely benefit to ultimate consumer viz. cost reduction, savings, efficient usage of resources etc. Many funds are registered as Social Venture Funds for Start Ups having greater social impact.

For understanding the efficiency of the "Start Up" India action plan, it is worth looking back at Small Industry Development Bank of India (SIDBI's) experience in funding Start Ups. SIDBI has been supporting Start Ups and early stage enterprises through contribution to various venture funds and has so far supported 88 different funds and has assisted 612 units, out of which 530 were MSMEs.

The Fund of Funds architecture, galvanizes inclusive growth, driven by innovative and disruptive business models of assisted units, while providing employment to educated and skilled youths. Flow of private capital will inject greater resilience in the ecosystem. It is proving to be one of the efficient financial leveraging structures compared other contemporary PPP models.

Other Initiatives

❖ Startup Fests

The government will implement various measures for promoting research and innovation among students.

❖ Innovation Centres at National Institutes

The government will set up 35 new incubators, 31 innovation centres at national institutes. Seven new research parks – six in IITs and one in IISc shall be set up by the government with an initial investment of ₹ 100 crore each.

❖ Biotechnology Boost

Five new bio clusters, 50 new bio incubators, 150 technology transfer offices and 20 bio connect offices will be established.

❖ Innovation Core {Programmes for Students}

It shall be launched to target school children in 5 lakh schools. Out of the total innovations from school children, the best 100 would be selected and are showcased at the Annual Festival of Innovations in the Rashtrapati Bhavan.

❖ Nidhi

The National Initiative for Developing and Harnessing Innovations is a grand challenge programme to support and award 10 lakh rupees to 20 student innovations from Innovation and Entrepreneurship Development Centres (IEDCs).

❖ Uchhattar Avishkar Yojana

It is a joint programme of Ministry of HRD and Department of Science and Technology that aimed at fostering 'very high quality' research among IIT students. The scheme will make a bridge between the academics and the practical working on field.

❖ Annual Incubator Grand Challenge

This will be launched to select 10 incubators who have the potential to become world class. The government plans ₹ 10 crore assistance for them to ramp up capacity.

Critical Evaluation of the Schemes

A tax break of three years has been given in the scheme. Anyone who has business sense knows that only a few of Start Ups will be profitable in the first three years and so this handful can avail themselves of the tax break.

When it comes to the 'fund of funds' under the initiative, ₹ 500 crore has already been provided as fund corpus in 2015-16 and ₹ 600 crore has been earmarked for 2016-2017. Cumbersome procedures to access funds from the ₹ 10, 000 Cr. corpus have, however, made the plan a non-starter and SIDBI has committed only ₹ 129 crore to VCs so far so the progress has been slow.

Under the scheme, bank only puts in 15% of the total corpus, while it is the VC that has to bring the remaining 85% to the table. And, this year, VCs have struggled to raise that kind of money—as a result, funding has almost halved.

There is also the government's requirement that participating investors have to be registered with the Securities and Exchange Board of India. But some of the biggest VCs aren't, and the government has essentially shut them out.

There is still no exemption in MAT (Minimum Alternate Tax) which could've helped businesses to cut losses.

A lot of entrepreneurs and investors think that demonetization and the lack of exits in Start Ups by investors are adding to the gloom; after demonetization, the investors are afraid to exit their investment due to slump in the IPO (Initial Public Offering) market.

The scheme sets up an 'Inter-Ministerial Board' led by the Department of Industrial Policy and Promotion which 'validates' the innovative nature of an enterprise, thereby qualifying it as a Start Up – an involvement of government in this ecosystem that is hardly desirable.

It also exempts starts-up from inspection under a fixed number of labour laws — six to be specific. But, there are about

45 laws at the central level and about four times this number at the state level. The Centre needs to work with the States to ensure a smooth rollout of the benefits under the Action Plan and avoid discord between policies at the two levels.

The Action Plan requires an enterprise or partnership to be innovative by developing and commercializing a new product or service — a step to promote truly innovative ideas. But it institutes an inter-ministerial body led by DIPP to examine whether an enterprise is 'innovative'.

It also requires a 'recommendation' from an incubator setup by the government or be supported by an incubator in a post-graduate institution recognized by the government — this need for validation and recommendation goes against the very steps the Action Plan takes to reduce government involvement. This additional layer of bureaucracy could slow down the starting up process and needs to go.

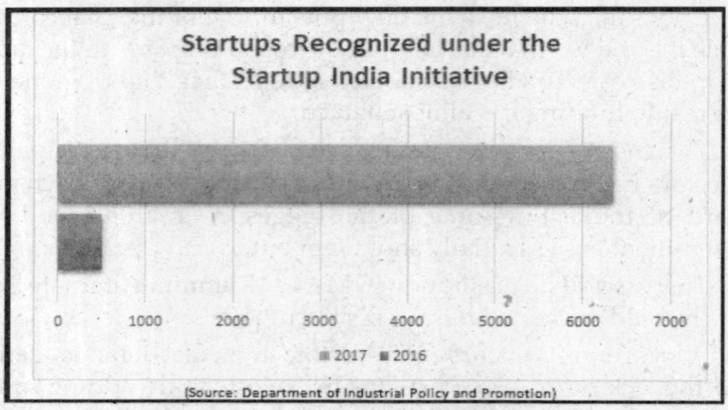

(Source: Department of Industrial Policy and Promotion)

Conclusion

While initiatives like Start Up certification, roping in bodies like CBDT to give tax breaks to entrepreneurs, setting up incubators and tinkering labs have been lauded there is a lot more that could have been done. While the progress is slow, the ecosystem feels much supported as the government put light on their struggles and achievements. However, there is a lot more that can be done in programming and implementation of Start Up India action plan.

Start Up India is consistent with the PM's call for innovation when he launched Digital India. The Start Up India Action plan is a good start to this – but will need continued support and evolution to make this a true, deep revolution for the youth of India.

India must have a strategy to unleash the potential of youth to provide meaningful opportunities for their participation in the growth journey, thereby fueling its economic growth targets. All these necessitate our growth model to be not only inclusive, accommodative and participative but also employment-centric. This will help us reap benefits of favorable demography, besides providing direct and effective intervention to remove despondency among millions of marginalized citizens and would uplift their quality of lives.

These two initiatives duly nestled with drives like MUDRA, Make in India and Digital India, would fuel India's pace to achieve long cherished goals of highly participative, universally inclusive and delightfully desirable economic ambiance.

❑❑❑

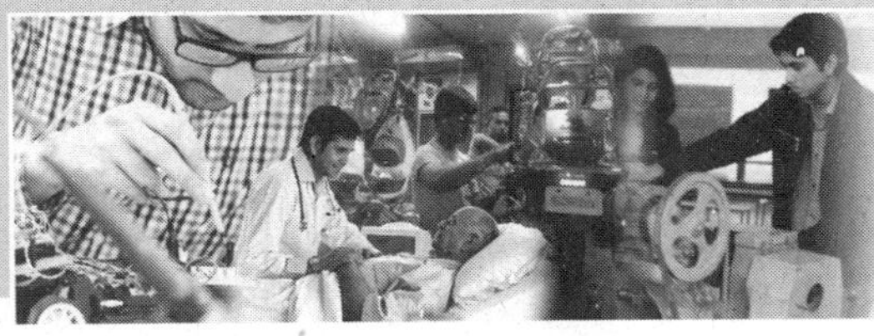

Chapter

7

Atal Tinkering Labs Igniting India's School Children

'Innovation' is the buzzword in the current Indian polity — and rightly so. Slow and steadily gaining traction and favoured by Prime Minister Narendra Modi, the Government of India has involved several ministries to support innovation schemes — especially for schemes like 'Start-up India' and 'Make in India'.

Ideally, the innovation process requires having an idea. In order to inculcate the concept of 'idea' among students to think and learn, the country's think-tank NITI Aayog under the Ministry of Human Resource and Development started to facilitate the setting up of Atal Tinkering Lab (ATL) in both government and private run-schools and institutes an year ago.

What is a tinkering lab?

In the context of education, the tinkering lab refers to space where the youngsters can experiment with, learn, develop and conceptualize different scientific ideas. It is a lot similar to DIY method where the students are encouraged to apply the knowledge that they have gained in the classroom. It not only helps the students to learn the real life application and importance of the theories they have learned from their books but will also develop a natural affinity towards STEM. In fact, science is something to be "felt and experienced" rather than reading and learning. The Newton did not "learn" about gravity in books but "experienced" the apple falling upon his head that led him to discover the law of gravity. In the same way, the Archimedes law was discovered when the mathematician was taking a bath and observed that sitting inside a bathtub resulted in the displacement of water, something that eventually led to Archimedes law. So, if the students are offered the ideal ambiance and tools for practically experiencing the theories they learned in the classroom, they would also be encouraged to dig deeper and innovate something new.

Atal Innovation Mission (AIM)

Atal Innovation Mission (AIM) including Self-Employment and Talent Utilization (SETU) is Government of India's endeavour to promote a culture of innovation and entrepreneurship. Its objective is to serve as a platform for promotion of world-class Innovation Hubs, Grand Challenges, Start-up businesses and other self-employment activities, particularly in technology driven areas. What AIM is doing is opening tinkering labs in schools and this will put everything from robots to IOT at the hands of students from class 6 and above.

❖ The Atal Innovation Mission shall have two core functions

- Entrepreneurship promotion through Self-Employment and Talent Utilization, wherein innovators would be supported and mentored to become successful entrepreneurs
- Innovation promotion; to provide a platform where innovative ideas are generated
- Atal Tinkering Labs
- Atal Incubation Centers
- Scale-up support to Established Incubators

Atal Tinkering Labs

With a vision to 'Cultivate one Million children in India as Neoteric Innovators', Atal Innovation Mission is started by Modi, it is establishing Atal Tinkering Laboratories (ATLs) in schools across India. The objective of this scheme is to foster curiosity, creativity and imagination in young minds; and inculcate skills such as design mindset, computational thinking, adaptive learning, physical computing etc.

❖ Key Features of ATL

ATL is a work space where young minds can give shape to their ideas through hands on do-it-yourself mode; and learn innovation skills. Young children will get a chance to work with tools and equipment to understand the concepts of STEM (Science, Technology, Engineering and Math). ATL would contain educational and learning 'do it yourself' kits and equipment on – science, electronics, robotics, open source microcontroller boards, sensors and 3D printers and computers. Other desirable facilities include meeting rooms and video conferencing facility.

In order to foster inventiveness among students, ATL can conduct different activities ranging from regional and national level competitions, exhibitions, workshops on problem solving, designing and fabrication of products, lecture series etc. at periodic intervals.

❖ Financial Support

AIM will provide grant-in-aid that includes a one-time establishment cost of ₹ 10 lakh and operational expenses of ₹ 10 lakh for a maximum period of 5 years to each ATL.

The lab will offer dedicated work spaces where students from Classes VI to XII can learn innovation skills and develop ideas that will help in the transformation of India.

❖ Present Status

The first phase of Atal Tinkering Labs brought India a step closer to the mission of Creating One Million Neoteric Child Innovators in India by 2020. 2441 schools across the country have been selected to establish an Atal Tinkering Lab. ATLs will be hubs of innovation where young minds will accelerate their ideas to solve unique local problems. The lab activities are designed to spur the spark of creativity, and go beyond regular curriculum and text book learning. The labs will let students explore the skills of future such as design and computational thinking, adaptive learning and artificial intelligence.

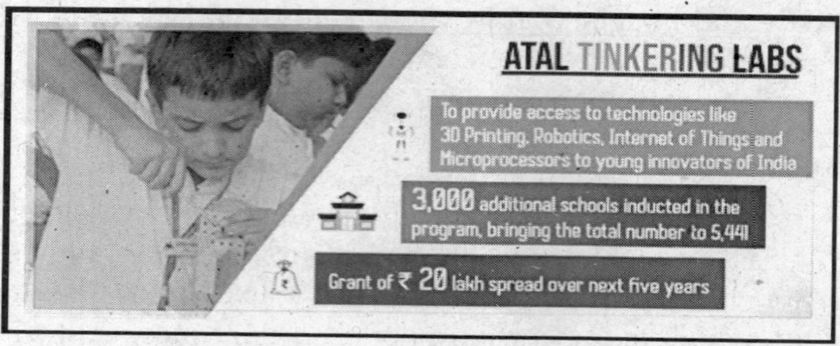

Government has roped-in as many as 5,000 individual mentors to guide students. In addition, it is partnering with global technology giants having significant investment in emerging technologies. So far, Atal Innovation Mission has signed agreements with American technology giants IBM, Intel and on 27th March, 2018, it signed a Statement of Intent (SOI) with the German enterprise software maker SAP.

According to SOI, SAP will set-up 100 labs across Delhi, Rajasthan, Gujarat, Maharashtra, Karnataka, Andhra Pradesh and Telangana by 2018-19, out of which about 50 labs are already operational. Under this programme, SAP employees will volunteer to coach and mentor students in advanced technology topics, and the design lab of SAP Labs India, will provide training and allow students to gain hands-on experience with technology gadgets. SAP will also provide CSR grants through non-profit partners. These partnerships are a win-win situation and this is possible only through effective public-private partnership.

Why do we need Atal Tinkering labs in schools?

STEM is a group of subjects that could get quite monotonous if taught in a cubicle classroom with the help of textbooks. These subjects, because of their very structure, are complex and may also appear convoluted.

- The theories, principles, properties, theorems and various tenets presented by STEM may seem convoluted for many students. So, they generally take an easy way and simply mug up these things during examination time.
- No wonder many of the high-grade students are unable to remember even the basic STEM texts and reference they read in lower grades.
- Because of the above points, the foundation of STEM is quite weak in many students and over a period of time they are detached from the subject (s) due to limited loyalty.
- One of the major challenges posed by traditional classroom learning (through textbooks) is that even the students that are able to join the relevant fields of engineering, science or mathematics are limited to professional requirements of the job rather than developing an innovative approach.
- The lack of innovative approach in STEM subjects limits the candidates from taking full advantage of their potential.
- While working with relevant tools and helpful ambiance, the students are able to learn the complex aspects of STEM subjects in a more direct and human way.
- Engaging multiple senses for practically experiencing the concepts of STEM subjects help the students to retain the different aspects of the topics.

- Do-It-yourself ambiance helps the students to develop a natural inclination towards "innovating" rather than sticking to the limitations of learned words.
- The very structure of Tinkering labs allows the students to perfectly blend the left (logical) and right (creative) brain. It helps the students to develop a natural "liking" towards their subjects.

❖ Benefits to school children

ATL is an approach of Modi's government which will create an environment of scientific temperament, innovation and creativity amongst Indian students. It is a step towards a New India by Modi.

ATL lab would teach students essential 21st-century skills which will help them in developing their professional and personal skills. As envisioned by Modi, Skilled India is the need of the hour and this dream will come true if we work towards it.

The objective of this scheme is to foster curiosity, creativity, and imagination in young minds and inculcate skills such as design mindset, computational thinking, adaptive learning, physical computing etc. Young children will get a chance to work with tools and equipment to understand what, how and why aspects of STEM (Science, Technology, Engineering and Math).

ATL is a workspace where young minds can give shape to their ideas through hands-on do-it-yourself mode and learn innovation skills. The vision is to cultivate 1 Million children in India as Neoteric Innovators.

As Innovation has been gaining importance, in order to further improve the skills of young minds a platform is needed and ATL will fill this requirement. The schools for the purpose are selected from different geographical areas and different managements. This will also help in capacity building of school teachers and their hands will be strengthened, who in turn help the students to sharpen their creative minds.

The approach is aimed at eliminating the limitations caused by monotonous classroom learning and using only textbooks as a reference without any exposure to a practical approach. The students would work with the specific tools and equipment to explore the practical relevance of STEM theories and concepts.

In order to further encourage the children to exhibit their acquired talent, the timely competitions will also be held where students can exhibit their skills and talent in the form of various relevant projects.

As opposed to the textbook-module of learning that could limit the interest of many students because of its monotonous character, the ATL will offer a perfect ambiance for the students to practice their acquired knowledge and work with relevant tools that are specifically designed to exhibit the foster creativity.

❖ Case study

For almost a month now, six students— Pallavi Solanki, Ankush Soni, Aadit Patel, Siddharth Jadeja and Mitesh Suthar of class XI (Science) and Jatin Dabhi of class IX—have been mentoring students of other schools, living near their homes showing them how to assemble a robotic car or putting together an electric circuit to make an LED bulb work. Their school, Sheth Amulakh Vidyalaya, was among the six from city chosen for Atal Tinkering Lab (ATL), a part of Atal Innovation Mission (AIM) which is an initiative by government under the Niti Aayog. Across India, 941 schools were selected for ATL where students get an opportunity to work with tools and equipment that help them understand concepts of Science, Technology, Engineering and Math (STEM). The ATL at their school became operational in 2016. "Students of other schools are not lucky enough to have teachers helping them learn robotics and other advanced subjects. It is the responsibility of the privileged to help those who are not," says Pallavi.

❖ Conclusion

We live in 21st Century world where change is constant and learning never stops. The new learners inside schools need a broad range of experiences to prepare for challenges of dynamic work environments, as well as to ensure the ongoing innovation and entrepreneurship. We believe the New Media & Technology can empower our children to not only communicate ideas & information more effectively, but also to generate new ideas, products, and processes.

Hence the need of the hour is to make our children Future Ready by teaching them the 21st Century skills like Design Thinking, and the universally acceptable language of Visual Communication with the help of Technology Tools of Creativity and Imagination. With the advent of Atal Tinkering Labs, the Indian education system is all poised to join the revolution that is aimed at converting young minds into thinkers and innovators. The students would develop a more dedicated approach towards STEM subjects and would also be inclined towards innovation as the model fosters a DIY (Do It Yourself) approach under able supervision. The students would learn the real life relevance of STEM subjects and would also learn to associate various concepts and principles that would further broaden their horizons.

Amitabh Kant, CEO of NITI Aayog, asserts that India's growth for the next few decades will depend on the innovations coming out of these tinkering labs. "Tomorrow's ideas come from students, who will disrupt industries and creative sectors with new technologies and processes which will thrust India into the leadership position for technological creativity and innovation…". Passing on of knowledge down to the grassroots levels of society was the aim behind the programme.

❑❑❑

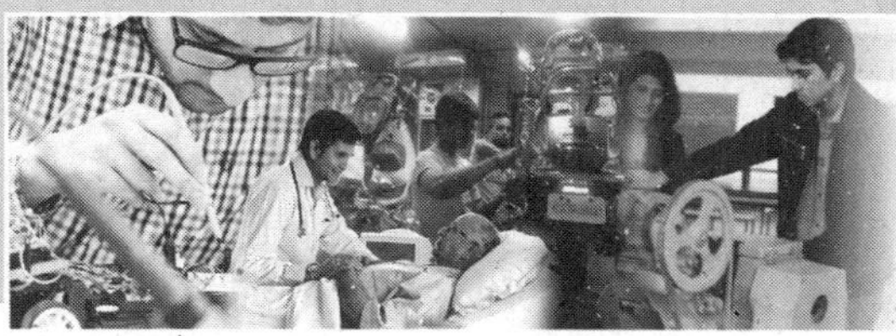

Chapter 8

Role of an NGO in the Field of Skill Development

During launching the National Mission for Skill Development 2015, Indian Prime Minister, Narendra Modi acknowledged that 'India currently faces a severe shortage of well-trained, skilled workers. It is estimated that only 2.3 per cent of the workforce in India has undergone formal skill training'. An NGO should make efforts in this direction and provide them skill-development training so that they can tackle ever-emerging economic challenges. An NGO should offer them vocational skill training, promote entrepreneurship and development of micro enterprises. An NGO should provide appropriate placement support to men and women, in tune with current market needs and demands along with updated skill-development training. To increase awareness and self-confidence among women, an NGO should also focus in this direction and mobilize women to form self-help groups, where they would collectively work and fulfil their household requirements through income. They need to be involved in financially productive businesses such as Broom-making, *Silai-Kadhai*, Sanitary Napkin making, Mushroom Farming, Pickle and *Papad* Making, *Dona-Pattal* Making and many others based on geographical location and demand. The women also need to be linked with local markets so that they could sell their products at a profit and earn money for the SHG. The habit of saving with knowledge of bank transaction is needed to be encouraged.

Through the Integrated Livelihood Development Programmes, the challenge of unemployment and underemployment need to be carefully tackled along with improving the quality of life for the community. One step ahead, financial literacy sessions should be organized to familiarize the community members with the know-how of financial transactions.

NGOs are often needed to fulfil the gaps left by the government. India has a large population that is at risk–in terms of health, education, jobs and opportunities in general. India has 3.3 million NGOs, or say, one NGO for every 400 individuals, so a large proliferation of NGOs can be seen. Many NGOs setup in India are either dormant or fraudulent, used for a wide range of illegal activities like tax evasion and misappropriation of government funds. But, there are some credible NGOs that do beneficial work for the people, providing important services–from education to health and disaster management to pet care, these NGOs play a positive role in every sector of the nation's economy.

Due to the abundance of capable, flexible and qualified human capital, India has gradually evolved as a knowledge-based economy. To ensure the country's global competitiveness, there is a need to further develop and empower the human capital. Despite working a lot on the education and training of people in the nation, there is still a shortage of skilled manpower to fulfil the needs and demands of the economy. Presently, there are at least 20 different government bodies in India running skill development programmes with less effort and huge duplication of work. For example, both the Ministry of Labour and Employment (MoLE) and the Ministry of Human Resource Development (MHRD) created their own sector skill councils last year to identify skill development requirements in the country, even the NSDC has been setting up Sector Skill Councils since 2011. In addition, to reduce policy confusion, apprenticeship system,

Labour Market Information System (LMIS) implementation, private sector coordination, etc., should be housed exclusively within one agency.

NGOs have become quite effective in the field of national development in recent decades. The vast category of groups and organizations are involved in NGOs. The UN's report on civil society describes NGO as: 'All organizations of relevance to the United Nations that are not central governments and were not created by intergovernmental decision, including associations of businesses, parliamentarians and local authorities. There is considerable confusion surrounding this term in United Nations circles. A civil society organization (CSO) is formally constituted to provide a benefit to the general public or the world at large through the provision of advocacy or services. They include organizations devoted to environment, development, human rights and peace and their international networks. They may or may not be membership-based'.

Because of being small and horizontally structured with short lines of communication, majority of NGOs are capable of responding rapidly to clients' requirements and changing circumstances. Also, NGOs have such work ethics that make generating sustainable processes and impacts possible. NGOs linkage with the rural poor enables them to maintain a field presence in remote locations and one of the main concerns of the NGO is to identify the needs of the rural poor in sustainable agricultural development. They have pioneered a wide range of participatory methods for diagnosis and have developed systems for testing new technology. The rapport that NGOs share with locals has been instrumental in integrating systems of local knowledge in the design of technology options and strengthening them by ensuring that the technologies developed are reintegrated into them. NGOs have also developed innovative dissemination methods, relying on farmer-to-farmer contact, whether on a group or individual basis. The culture of working in group is one of the main strengths of NGOs, which can be adjusted or altered as per the need at various levels. Thus, to attain simultaneous action in skill development programme, Action for World Solidarity in India started working with grass-roots organizations.

Role of NGOs as skill development intermediaries is given below:

- They are able to reach and mobilize the poor and far-off communities;
- They help empower poor people to improve their lives by offering skill development courses and promoting entrepreneurship, and they work with and strengthen local institutions;
- They work on projects with lower costs and more efficiently than the government agencies; and
- They promote sustainable development.

The community-focused approach is the main strength of NGOs, which will help to solve the issues related to skill development. This can be achieved with effective NGO cooperation. Where a majority of people live in different rural areas, NGOs makes it possible to supply aid to victims and initiating social restoration work in rural zones. For proper sharing of responsibility in the skill development process, efforts made by the government and NGOs to achieve coordination will prove effective. NGOs focus mostly on sector-specific issues like livelihood, community organization, community asset creation, women group formation, etc., and works for social and economic recovery after disasters. While the state follows a universalistic approach in supporting victims, NGOs could opt for community-oriented approach and serve to the needs of vulnerable groups who otherwise find it hard to cope with the modern world.

For determining the roles of states and businesses as well as operating as businesses themselves, NGOs will play an important role in the future. Some challenges before the non-government organization are mentioned below:

- Governments and business oppose their advocacy in developing and deploying solutions.
- This represents a challenge even for most mainstream NGOs, so public and private sector partnerships are increasingly essential in leveraging change.

- New forms of competition are evolving in the 'NGO market', with new entrants such as companies, business networks, NGO networks and social entrepreneurs blurring traditional boundaries.
- Both national and international NGOs have to focus in the whole area of branding and competitive positioning.
- Some steps needed for strengthening NGOs are mentioned here:
- State and NGOs should collaborate for proper functioning and overcome their differences for establishing greater synergy in efforts for minimum use of resources.
- There is also a requirement of making efforts at information sharing and social audit to strengthen transparency and accountability, which would raise their credibility.
- Setting minimum parameters for humanitarian aid and standardize people's rights and entitlements can clear the doubts about NGOs.
- Prepare adequate database on NGO skills, capacities, and resources and needs so that the government could identify the NGOs which would work in strengthening skills and capacities in community's development.
- Take steps to bridge 'learning gaps' by documenting disaster experiences and successful response stories for wider dissemination among people.
- NGOs should take steps to strengthen alliances and networking among themselves in order to align their initiatives in sustainable development.
- Finally, NGOs should bring some changes in their governance structure in order to strengthen their representative character and enhance their credibility among people and the government.

As India is one of the few countries across the world the working age population of which is very high, Skill India can prove to be a good initiative for providing skills to people. To improve the physical and mental development of the youths of the nation so that none of them remains unemployed and the country's unemployment problem gets reduced, these skill improvement measures are very important. It is time to create such opportunities by which the youth accepts responsibility and no one remains unemployed. The economy should mostly focus on job creation and social security programmes. Skill development is a great way through which India can definitely move forward towards becoming a developed nation. Technical expertise and innovative thinking may be of utmost importance for India in a quest to become a developed nation and thereby improving employability of learners. NGOs are doing brilliant work in different sectors for the growth of nation both socially and economically. For example in education sector, some of the most well-known NGOs would include Pratham (research on educational outcomes, famous for the Annual State of Education Report), Teach for India (direct intervention in low-income classrooms) and *Akshya-Patra* (involved with the mid-day meal scheme). Similarly, on the other side, NGOs like Goonj are involved with other issues that specially focus on clothing and believes that merely by reusing the existing clothing in the nation, one major problem of poverty can be eliminated. Moreover, a large number of NGOs are dealing with one of the most important issues facing the poor: Lack of quality skills and employment opportunities. These NGOs work on skill development programmes and livelihood creation by offering entrepreneurial opportunities for them. In future also, NGOs will continue to play a vital role in nation building. To make India a better place for disadvantaged sections of society, increase in both CSR spending and prosperity will play a vital role. There are maximum chances that NGOs would receive a large amount of funds in the future, for that the NGOs have to adopt best practices and bring about the maximum transparency through auditing and reporting. For instance, NGOs like *Akshya-Patra* have grown vastly in scale by regularly delivering results year after year. CSR spending will benefit only the most trustworthy organizations and allow them to grow in scale. Due to this trend, larger and more responsible NGOs will be able to deliver results more effectively and efficiently, making best use of resources. Thus, NGOs will continue to play a very important and beneficial role in Indian society, but it is also important for NGOs to open themselves for auditing and reporting.

❑❑❑

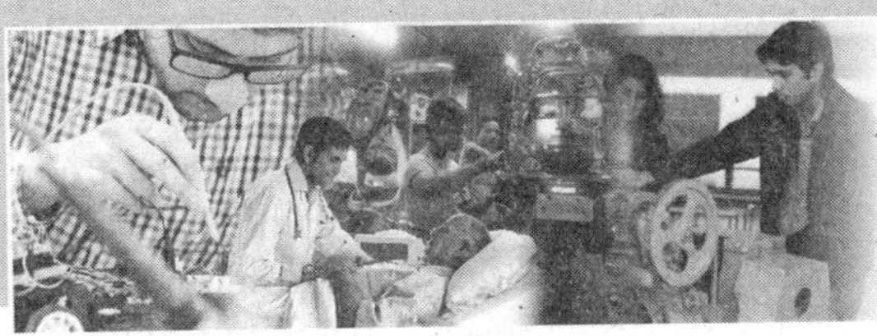

Chapter

9

Modi's achievements on Employment Opportunities in India

The Government of India under the able guidance of Hon'ble Prime Minister Mr. Narendra Modi is following the approach of 'Reform to Transform' through far-reaching structural reforms being committed to job security, wage security and social security for each and every one.

Employment Generation is the first priority for Modi Government. After going through a decade of jobless growth, government is working on a comprehensive strategy to bring employment to the core of nation's development. Promoting industrial activity through Make in India, ; enhancing employability through Skill India and encouraging innovation and entrepreneurship through Start up India and Standup India, are a few examples of transformative initiatives that government has taken in last 4 years.

From Skill India programme to Digital India and Make in India, and from Swachh Bharat Mission to Shyama Prasad Mukherji Rurban Mission, PM Narendra Modi has launched around 30 flagship programmes in the last three years to generate jobs and improve ease of doing business in India.

Present Employment Status in last 4 years

Government released a book on the achievements and initiatives of the Ministry of Labour and Employment during the last three years, announced various programmes for job creation. The report said over 3.87 crore candidates and 14.8 lakh establishments had registered on the National Career Service (NCS) portal which has mobilised over six lakh vacancies. It also cited that around 540 job fairs had been organised in 2016-17.

Apart from this, the Pradhan Mantri Rojgar Protsahan Yojana had been announced to incentivise employers for new employment. "Government will be paying the 8.33% Employees Pension Scheme contribution for these new employees for a period of three years. For the textile (apparel and made-up) sector, government will also pay the 3.67% employees provident fund contribution of employers for these new employees. Till now, benefits have been transferred to 1,954 establishments covering 75,848 beneficiaries under the scheme with an expenditure of ₹ 6 crores."

If we just look at EPFO data, over 45 lakh formal jobs were created between September 2017 to April 2018. According to our study based on EPFO data, over 70 lakh jobs were created in the formal sector alone last year. We all know that informal sector constitutes around 80% of all jobs. We also know that creation of jobs in the formal sector has a spin off effect on job creation in the informal sector. There are more than 15,000 start-ups which the Government has helped and as we all know they are job multipliers. More than 13 crore people were given loans under MUDRA Scheme.

Nearly 1.2 crore jobs were created in the country in the 10-month period till June this year, as per a Central Statistics Office (CSO) report. The CSO's employment outlook report is based on the new member enrolments with retirement fund body EPFO, Employees' State Insurance Scheme (ESI) and NPS. According to the report, as many as 1,19,66,126 new members joined the health insurance scheme Employers State Insurance (ESI) of the ESIC during September 2017 to June 2018, with highest number of new member enrolments in May this year at 13,18,395.

Similarly, as many as 1,07,54,348 new members joined the Employment Provident Fund Organisation (EPFO) while 60,40,616 persons ceased to be its members during the 10-month period. The estimated total number of new NPS (National Pension Scheme) subscribers during the period is 6,10,573, the report said.

Government developed a National Career Service Portal to facilitate the youth to get information of availability of suitable jobs. 100 Model Career Centres are being established across the country that will guide youth of India to the employment opportunity and related career counseling. So far 35 million job seeking youth and 1 million employers have registered on this platform.

As many as 8.5 million young people have got jobs under the government's flagship employment generation scheme, the Pradhan Mantri Rojgar Protsahan Yojana (PMRPY).

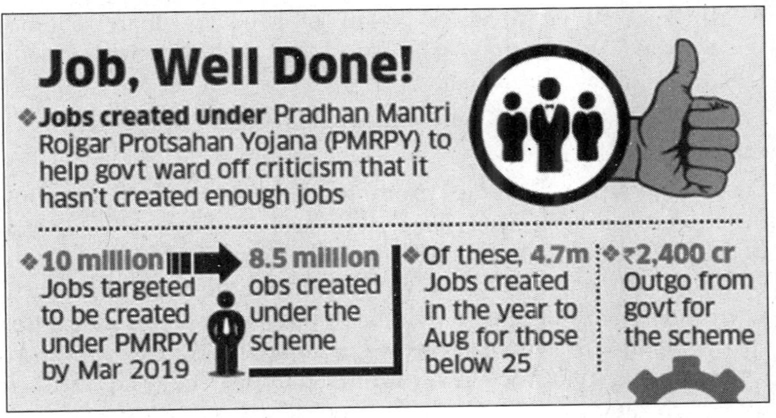

Source: Ministry of Labour and Employment

Modi's programs for job creation

Guaranteed Wage Employment – MGNREGA Mahatma Gandhi National Rural Employment Guarantee Act (MGNREGA) was enacted in 2005, with the aim to enhance livelihood security of the households in rural areas of the country by providing at least 100 days of wage employment in a financial year to every household whose adult members volunteer to do unskilled manual work.

Startup India Program: An Initiative for Innovation and Inclusiveness

- Startup India mission will ease the transition from education to employment for a youngster while nurturing innovative mindset.
- It aims to promote entrepreneurship, innovation and inclusive development at all the levels of economic growth and social development process.
- This is the platform where creative and innovative youth will get a forum to translate their dreams into reality.

Promoting indigenous handicraft industries

- Providing Skill Development Training for Carpets weaving.
- Setting up of Indian Institute of Carpet Technology (IICT) at Bhadohi.
- Interest subvention and grant of MUDRA loan schemes to the handicrafts artisans so as to compete with machine-made products.
- Organizing Indian Handicrafts & Gifts Fair twice a year

Stand up India Scheme

Stand Up India Scheme promotes entrepreneurship among Scheduled Castes/Scheduled Tribes and Women. The scheme provides for composite loans by banks between ₹ 10 lakh and upto ₹ 100 lakh for setting up a new enterprise in the non-farm sector. These loans would be eligible for refinance and credit guarantee cover. There will also be a credit guarantee fund of ₹ 5,000 crore for providing guarantee cover for loans under Stand Up India in first five years.

❖ Creating Employment through Skill Development

Micro Units Development Refinance Agency (MUDRA) Bank: It has been established with an aim to encourage entrepreneurs to set up micro units. The Bank will refinance Micro-Finance Institutions through a Pradhan Mantri Mudra Yojana and will have a corpus of ₹ 20,000 crore, and credit guarantee corpus of ₹ 3,000 crore. Priority would be given to SC/ST enterprises while lending since these bottom-of-the-pyramid, hard-working entrepreneurs (SC/ST) find it difficult, if not impossible, to access formal systems of credit. Hence, these measures will greatly increase the confidence of young, educated or skilled workers who will now be able to aspire to become first generation entrepreneurs.

Deen Dayal Upadhyay Gramin Kaushal Yojana

It has been launched to cater to rural youth employment opportunities. Disbursement will be through a digital voucher directly into qualified student's bank account.

SETU (Self Employment and Talent Utilisation)

SETU is a Techno Financial, Incubation and Facilitation Programme to support all aspects of start-up businesses, and other self-employment activities, particularly in technology-driven areas.

Atal Innovation Mission (AIM)

AIM is an Innovation Promotion Platform involving academics, entrepreneurs, and researchers and draw upon national and international experiences to foster a culture of innovation, R&D and scientific research in India. The platform will also promote a network of world-class innovation hubs and Grand Challenges for India.

Self Employment in Horticulture

Government provides money (up to 10.00 Lac) for this venture by which one can start the Agriculture Clinic. By the funds provided, an educated horticulturist expert can raise commercial nursery of fruit plants, flower and ornamental plants. It can also facilitate the Seed producer of vegetables and flower crops, Fruit/Vegetable/Flower grower, Floral decorator/florist shop, Horticulture Services Contractor, Mushroom grower, Seed dealer/Merchant, Proprietor cold storage, Processing work of horticulture production and one can also establish an institute for vocational education.

National Rural Livelihood Mission (NLRM) / Aajeevika

It is designed as a special programme for rural development. For basic skill development of the BPL rural youth, the Rural Self Employment Institutes (RSETIs) under NRLM have been set up, which enables them to undertake micro enterprises and wage employment.

Make in India Programme

Through Make in India programme, the government intends to create 100 million new jobs by 2022 providing manufacturing sector a stronger role in domestic job creation. It has a goal of transforming the country into a global manufacturing hub.

Ease of Doing Business

The reforms include the following:

- The corporate tax rate for companies registered in India to go down from 30% to 25% of net profits in a phased manner.
- Goods and Services Tax has been implemented.
- Operationalising the e-BIZ portal.

Reforms taken by Modi for creating employment opportunities: Narendra Modi government has tried to address the problems of the informal sector through a focused approach which rests on two legs. The first is to promote formalisation and the second is the provision of social security to those remaining in the informal sector.

The most important reform is the introduction of "fixed term contract" employment. According to the notification introducing it, fixed contract workers must be employed under the same working conditions (such as wages, working hours, allowances and other benefits) as permanent workers. Allowing fixed-term employment would help employers to respond to the fluctuating demand and seasonality in their businesses and facilitate the direct employment of workers.

Under the Ease of Compliance rules, the government has pruned the number of registers mandatory for all establishments to be maintained under nine central Acts to just five from 56, and the relevant data fields to 144 from 933. The government has also taken numerous technology-enabled transformative initiatives such as the Shram Suvidha Portal, universal account number (UAN) and national career service portal in order to reduce the complexity burden and ensure better accountability. In order to reduce the labour law compliance cost for start-ups, the central government has also managed to persuade state governments and Union Territories (UT) to allow self-certification and regulate inspection under six labour laws wherever applicable.

One of the major achievements of the government is the increased Employees' Provident Fund (EPF) coverage. The Employees' Enrolment Campaign (EEC) was launched by the government in January 2017 to enroll employees left out of the EPF and provided incentives to employers in the form of a waiver of administrative charges, nominal damages at the rate of Re 1 per annum and waiver of employees share, if not deducted. In this drive, close to 1.01 crore additional employees were enrolled with EPF Organisation between January to June 2017.

The construction sector employs the highest number of casual workers outside of agriculture. As a result of the massive campaign and effort by the Union of India, state governments and UTs, the approximate number of building and other construction workers registered as beneficiaries under Building and Other Construction Workers (BOCW) Act up to March 31 has increased to 3.06 crore. The most important reform for this sector is the introduction of Universal Access Number (UAN). If a construction worker migrates from one state to another (which is common), the benefit of registration will not be lost due to the portability of the UAN.

The amendment of the Payment of Wages Act in 2017 introduced a provision that the government may, by notification in the official gazette, specify that an industrial or other establishment shall pay wages only through its bank account. A notification to this effect with respect to the railways, air transport services, mines and oil field sectors covered under central sphere has been issued on April 25, 2017.

The government is also in the process of finalising Labour Code on Social Security. The Code aims to simplify, rationalise and consolidate the hitherto fragmented laws into one consolidated law, which will be simpler both in terms of comprehension and enforcement. The code has drawn inspiration from the Constitution and follows a rights-based approach.

Work is going on full swing in Mumbai-Delhi, Ludhiana-Kolkata, Vizag-Chennai, Chennai-Bengaluru and Bengaluru-Mumbai. The Government proposed to take up a few more industrial corridors in the coming years including extension of Vizag-Chennai corridor to Kolkata on one side and up to Tuticorin on the other side. All these will create the ambience for more small scale industrial clusters.

The digitization of the economy, hastened by demonetisation and rollout of Goods and Services Tax too will result in more jobs. Demonetisation will result in improving ease of doing business without corruption. The GST will push up GDP growth by a couple of percentage points.

Conclusion

Modi government has taken several initiatives during the last three years that will give the much needed boost to job creation. The results might not be evident immediately but it has certainly done the ground work for it. The more than doubling of highways construction, speeding up of rural roads development, spending of ₹ 8.5 lakh crore on capital expenditure in railways in the next five years, metro rail projects, all will push employment. Also allowing 100 per cent FDI in food processing will create more jobs in rural India apart from ensuring that ₹ 40,000 crore of fruits and vegetables that rot every year is drastically reduced. This will also ensure better remuneration to farmers as well and create alternative occupation to rural population in their own backyard.

The Mudra scheme has ensured that several crores of youth got jobs through self employment. The youth of rural India not only get jobs for themselves but also become employers for few others in their start-ups. Improved connectivity through better infrastructure has ensured more industrial corridors to come in the country, which in turn will create more industrial clusters like Tiruppur in Tamil Nadu, Moradabad in Uttar Pradesh, Ludhiana in Punjab, Surat in Gujarat and Murshidabad in West Bengal.

Food Processing parks in areas where farm produce is abundantly available will ensure rural jobs and better income to farmers.

The Modi government's stress on clean energy, particularly solar power including roof-top power generation will ensure a lot of jobs for skilled and semi skilled workers. This is already visible in states like Tamil Nadu, Rajasthan, Andhra Pradesh, Gujarat, Karnataka where wind and solar power development have taken a big leap forward.

There might have been some hiccups in the short run in job creation because of these systemic and structural reforms but they have kick-started the sagging economy and created necessary base for big jump in employment generation in the coming years.

❑❑❑

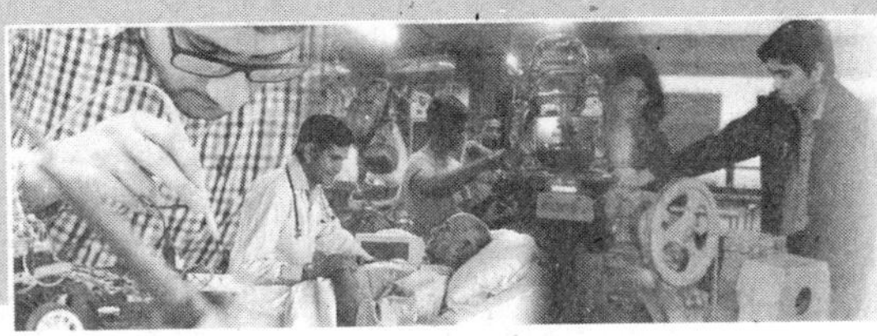

Chapter 10

Role of Urban Economic Development and Urban Policy of India: Challenges and Opportunities

The urban population is growing in India and because of this, opportunities are increasing as well. According to the country data, urbanization in India is mainly due to the expansion of cities and migration of people. Investments are made in housing, road network, urban transport, water supply, power-related infrastructures, smart cities, and other forms of urban management. This is the bright future the Indian economy has in store for itself. About 34% of India's population now lives in urban areas, the U.N. World Urbanization Prospects 2018 report has said. There is an increase of about three percentage points since the 2011 Census.

Importance of Urban Economic Development

Urbanization has been an essential part of most of the nations' development towards a stronger and more stable economy. The countries in the South that urbanized most rapidly in the last 10–

20 years are generally those with the most rapid economic growth. Most of the world's largest cities are counted as the world's largest economies, which is further an evidence of this link between economic wealth and cities. Cities and towns also have important roles in social transformation. They are centers of artistic, scientific and technological innovations, culture and education. Cities play an important role in economic development. Cities provide economies of scale, agglomeration, and localisation; they provide efficient infrastructure and services through density and concentration in transportation, communications, power, human interactions, water and sanitation services. They attract talented and skilled labor that allows specialization in knowledge, skills, and management capabilities.

Opportunities for Urban Economic Growth in India

- Private cities are now expanding due to the support of private companies. Private developers are building private housing projects that will exponentially grow in the years to come.
- The Delhi-Mumbai Corridor is an infrastructure program set to develop 'Smart Cities' and combine next-generation technology with infrastructural development.
- The transport and logistics sector of India underlines the importance of interconnecting the different modes of transportation: road, rail, sea and air. An efficient multi-modal system is relevant in the development and successful growth of the infrastructural systems.
- Special Economic Zones dot the landscape of India. Each of these zones is focused on a particular sector such as IT, apparel and fashion, or petroleum and petrochemical industries.
- Industrial townships are built to house employees close to the factories and manufacturing plants at which they work. After the success of the pioneering industrial township - Tata's Steel Town - the government is planning on developing more like it.
- India's expected economic growth opens up expansion prospects for Indian airports. Domestic and international passengers are inevitably predicted to double in number in the years to come.

Urban Economic Development Contribution to National Economy

Barclays Report: 2014

Urban India could house 35% of India's population and contribute 70-75% of its GDP by 2020, Barclays said in a report. India's urban sector presently constitutes 63% of India's GDP (that has risen up from 45% in 1990) and has been its key engine of growth acceleration in the past decade. With only 31% of India's population currently urbanized, along with high population density and low GDP per capita, India's urbanization trends have scope to significantly accelerate.

Urban Policy of India

❖ Ministry of Urban Development and Poverty Alleviation

The Centre has unveiled the Urban Development strategy for the next 20 years to use growing urbanization for rapid economic development. It will be achieved through elimination of barriers to the flow of factors of production like capital, land and labour, development of rural and urban areas in a synergetic manner adopting a 'regional planning approach', promoting inclusivity by ensuring urban services to all, sustainable urban planning, empowering municipalities to improve governance and deal with exclusion issues, housing for all urban poor and ensuring social justice and gender equity.

The government increased the budget for the housing and urban affairs ministry by 2.8%, to ₹ 41,765 crore. The centre has also formulated separate policies for urban sanitation, transport, transit-oriented development and also a national mission on sustainable habitat, each with a specific mandate and vision. The Government Seven Mission Program includes the following plans for cities:

- 100 Smart Cities Mission
- AMRUT stands for 'Atal Mission for Rejuvenation and Urban Transformation'
- HRIDAY (National Heritage City Development and Augmentation Yojana)

- Sardar Patel National Urban Housing mission
- National Mission on sustainable habitat
- Clean India mission
- National urban information system
- "Housing for All" mission, which aims to build 3 million houses in urban areas alone

❖ NITI

Niti Aayog in its 3 years strategy underlines the regulatory changes needed to push India on the path of faster urbanisation, which will boost the economy while helping absorb surplus agricultural labour. Urbanisation has hitherto been shackled by such a poor legal framework that even as India's urban population has grown over five decades, share of rental housing in overall housing has dropped. This can be remedied within a short period by freeing up laws governing rent controls, land ceilings, the floor space index and stamp duties. The Niti Aayog has also recommended releasing substantial chunks of urban land belonging to central and state governments that have remained unused or have been encroached upon. "These vacant lands can be monetised to provide affordable housing."

Budget 2018-19

Air pollution in Delhi and NCR

In his budget speech, Jaitley referred to a special scheme that would be implemented to support the efforts of the governments of Haryana, Punjab, Uttar Pradesh and the NCT of Delhi to address air pollution. Under the scheme, machinery required for in-situ management of crop residue would also be subsidised.

Urban schemes

Under the Prime Minister Awas Yojana, launched in both rural and urban areas to meet the objective of housing for all by 2022, assistance has been sanctioned to construct 37 lakh houses in urban areas in 2018-19.

A dedicated Affordable Housing Fund (AHF) would be earmarked in the National Housing Bank, funded from priority sector lending shortfall and fully serviced bonds authorized by the Government of India.

The Minister referred to 99 cities that have been selected with an outlay of ₹ 2.04 lakh crore under the Smart Cities Mission, under which projects like Smart Command and Control Centre, Smart Roads, Solar Rooftops, Intelligent Transport Systems, Smart Parks are in various stages of completion.

Under the Atal Mission for Rejuvenation and Urban Transformation (AMRUT), state level plans of ₹ 77,640 crore for 500 cities have been approved.

Water supply contracts for 494 projects worth ₹ 19,428 crore and sewerage work contract for 272 projects costing ₹ 12,429 crore have been awarded.

Credit rating for cities

The Economic Survey had already referred to the challenge of raising resources of the magnitude required to meet India's urbanisation imperative, especially given its commitment to the Sustainable Development Goals, 11 of which is to make "cities inclusive, safe, resilient and sustainable." To that end the Survey had suggested that Urban Local Bodies generate resources through financial instruments such as municipal bonds, PPPs and credit risk guarantees.

In his budget speech, the Finance Minister stated that 482 cities have started credit rating, and 144 cities have got investment grade rating.

The Mumbai-Bengaluru bonanza

Mumbai's local rail network is being expanded and augmented to add 90 kilometers of double line tracks at a cost of over ₹ 11,000 crore. 150 kilometres of additional suburban network is being planned at a cost of over ₹ 40,000 crore, including elevated corridors on some sections.

A suburban rail network of approximately 160 kilometres at an estimated cost of ₹ 17,000 crore is being planned for Bengaluru, as said by the Finance Minister.

India's first high speed rail project launched in September 2017, the Mumbai-Ahmedabad bullet train project, will also be benefited as an Institute is coming up at Vadodara that will train personnel to serve high speed rail projects.

Urban planning

Referring to higher education and augmentation of investments in research and related infrastructure in premier educational institutions, Jaitley said that the government would be setting up two new full-fledged Schools of Planning and Architecture (SPA), to be selected on challenge mode. Additionally, 18 new SPAs would be established in the IITs and NITs as autonomous Schools, also on challenge mode.

Challenges of Urban Economic Development in India

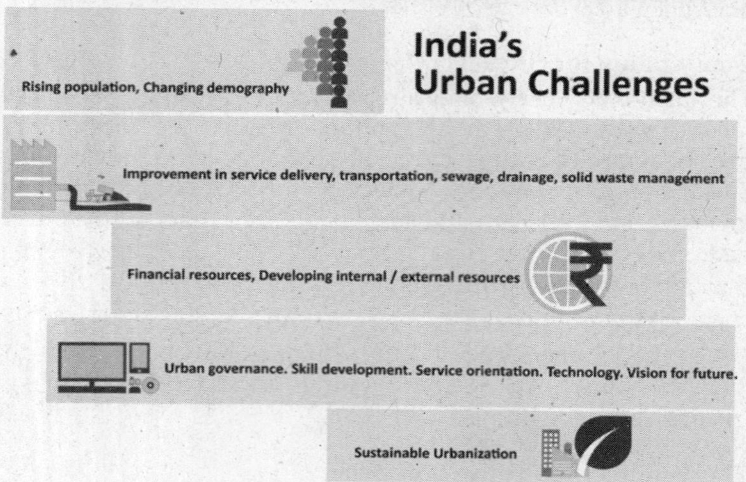

Source: Livemint

Woeful state of water and sanitation

Less than 50% of the population is covered adequately by municipal supplies of drinking water. The ground water/trucked water dependence has increased in most cities. The sewerage system covers well below 100% usually less than 70% of the population even in the very best of situations. Nowhere is the water quality good and there is almost no city where the supplies are 24x7. Wastage is as high as 40-60%.

STATE OF AFFAIRS IN CITIES

Indicators	National Average	Benchmark
Scientific disposal of municipal waste	9.7	100
Waste processed	14.5	80
Segregation of municipal waste	10.8	100
Collection of municipal waste	75.6	100
Sewage network coverage	12.2	100
Sewage treatment capacity	5.3	100
Storm water drain coverage	45.8	100
Toilet coverage	40.1	100
Continuity of water supply	3.1	24 hrs

*All figures in percentage

Source: Times of India

Unclean as can be

India has very high morbidity in the world and there is no part of the soil and dust of any city barring perhaps those in the North East, that is not contaminated by fecal matter. As many as 25% of the population do their toilet in the open in Mumbai's premium city making no part of the city free of the stench of human feces. Open defecation even in a well-managed city like Ahmedabad is common. There are 119 places in the city where open defection takes place. The high disease burden and bacterial load also adversely affects MMR, infant mortality death in hospitals and quality of life.

Electricity supplies have not improved

Quality of electricity supply varies from city to city and even more from location to location. Only Gujarat has near 24X7 supplies. Most other states would have their capital cities where the elites congregate with near 24 x 7 supplies, but most other cities have frequent power cuts making life in the summer months to most people unbearable when these cuts are on.

Even primary health care ails

Primary health care in urban India is patchy but in comparison to the failure in drinking water, sewerage and sanitation, it can be considered as better. In the cities of Tamil Nadu and Kerala, and in many cities in Karnataka and Maharashtra, state provision is passable, but in most others there is glaring failure. In some states like Bihar even inoculation programmes have not met their targets and there are large numbers of children who even today are victims of entirely avoidable diseases.

The chaos of transportation design

The share of private and para transport has increased everywhere. The share of potentially social value enhancing public transport has declined almost everywhere. The share of private motorized transport especially the ubiquitous two-wheeler has gone up sharply in urban India. In urban places with much higher per capita incomes – Delhi, Goa, Ernakulam, Ahmedabad etc., cars now do a significant part of the commuting.

Unaffordable real estate

The problem of high costs of housing and real estate spaces in Indian cities is well known. Thus, Mumbai, a city in a country of less than US$ 1300 per capita income, has one of the highest real estate prices. Not only in the downtown area which is very high priced, but even in the periphery the prices tend to be higher than in most other cities in the world. This makes the cost of housing, even of the most basic variety so utterly out of the reach of poor especially in the metropolitan cities like Bengaluru, Delhi, Pune and Mumbai. They are therefore forced to live in illegal spaces since the option of going to the periphery is often out of question given their need to access work opportunities.

Sustainable Development

The challenge is about ensuring sustainable development while taking advantage of economic growth that results from rapid urbanization in the country. For long, urbanization has been looked at from the limited perspective of providing basic services.

Lack of Urban development courses

Institutions in India are yet to fully recognize and award graduate degrees in municipal finance and urban economics. India has less than five reputed schools of urban planning, and often veterinary officers write municipal accounts in many cities and towns.

Way Forward: Need for National Urban Policy

What is truly required is a comprehensive framework that takes a holistic approach to the interrelated challenges that have an impact on the growth of cities. Sustainable urban development needs to be led by the central government working closely with state and local governments.

To address this, India needs to develop its own national urban policy (NUP) as an instrument for applying a coherent set of interventions in relation to the future growth of cities, in partnership with all stakeholders. Globally, around one-third of countries have a NUP in place.

First, such a policy will outline and highlight the importance and objectives of cities. We need to update our definition of urban areas, understand the importance of cities and what we can achieve through urbanization with responsive infrastructure.

Second, urbanization in India is a complex issue, with the majority of city-related issues being state subjects. States would have to take the lead in order to make cities vibrant economic centres. However, there is a need to build adequate capacities at the state/urban local bodies level to prepare cities for future challenges. The NUP would set the common minimum agenda, involving participation of all stakeholders.

Third, the world of the 21st century is substantially more complex than the traditional urban world of the 20th century when citizens, government and civil society were, to a large extent, the only stakeholders. The present urban scenario has new stakeholders who are more connected than ever. An NUP framework would recognize all these stakeholders and prevent cities from seeing through these participants. Once their presence is acknowledged, states and cities would be better placed to develop the right processes and systems to utilize the potential of these stakeholders.

Fourth, an NUP will provide a framework for states, which would be encouraged and nudged to adopt a state version of this policy. This should have network effects that would change and define the paradigm of urban development in 21st century India.

Conclusion

Wholehearted introduction and implementation of urban reforms spanning governance, planning and financing are required, but will alone not suffice. A sustained focus on crafting and re-inventing the economic strategy for cities is vital for the overall development of the city, including its infrastructure-oriented master plan. To do so, cities need to have the capacity and capability required to formulate these twin plans that intertwine the economic vision and strategy with the infrastructure-led master plan. Subsequently, city governments need to deliver on these plans in a time-bound manner through a tireless focus on execution, something most fall short on. A holistic strategy that pushes a spectrum of reforms and builds capacity at scale is the burning need of the hour.

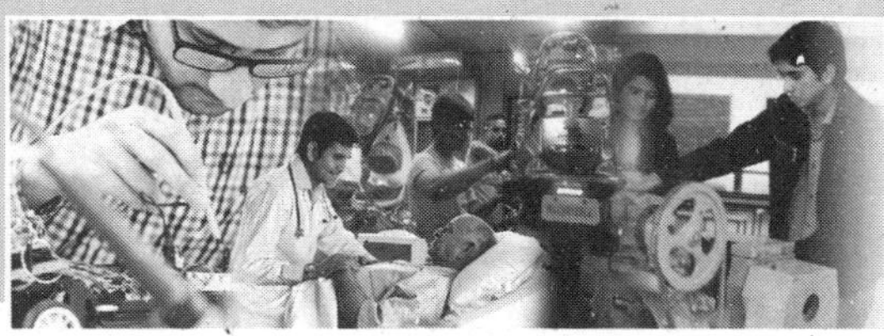

Chapter 11

Inclusive Policies and Affirmative Action

Seventy years later, the Modi government's policies have added an equality and inclusion-focused economic complement to the legal framework Babasaheb put in place. Zero-sum policies have been replaced with an inclusive growth agenda where everyone can benefit from a growing economic pie. Under the "sabka vikas" umbrella, the policy themes of economic security, equal opportunity and human dignity are strengthening the sense of ownership felt by citizens, and with it, unity.

Inclusive Policies of the government

❖ Poverty Reduction

With poverty alleviation forming the crux of the vision, the government led by PM Modi has been making rapid strides in eliminating poverty from the country. A recent report titled the 'The start of a new poverty narrative' published by a US think tank Brookings Institution, with data drawn from the World Data lab prepared by the World Bank, shows that India has achieved significant progress in combating poverty. The report highlights that the number of Indians living in abject poverty has fallen rapidly from 125 million in 2016 to 75 million today with a further fall to 20 million by 2022.

Identifying extreme poverty as living on less than ₹ 130.77 per day with reference to income per capita, India has made remarkable progress in reducing absolute poverty. With around '270 million people being poor where 1 in every five Indians was poor', according to the World Bank data produced in 2011, the number today stands at a glowing '70 million'. Besides, the faster reduction rate in poverty where close to '44 Indians come out of extreme poverty every minute', the decline in percentage in terms of absolute poverty has been significant. From registering a high '21.2 %' at the international poverty line in 2011, the percentage of people deprived in terms of absolute poverty stands today at mere '5.2 % of India's total population'. Further, according to the World Poverty clock that provides real-time poverty estimates until 2030, shows that 'India is currently on track of eliminating poverty by 2030' in tandem with the UN's Sustainable Development Goal of elimination of extreme poverty by 2030.

The government led by PM Modi has stressed on the concept of inclusive development that made the government's strategy of poverty alleviation a 'Jan Andolan' (mass movement). Subsumed under the principle of 'Antyodaya' which translates into 'empowering of the last man' the government in the past four years has undertaken striking reforms in multiple sectors spanning across economy, manufacturing , health, nutrition among others.

❖ Insurance: Jan Suraksha Yojana, Atal Pension Yojana and Fasal Bima Yojana and other such schemes

The Jan Suraksha Yojana scheme provides a rudimentary safety net to the most economically vulnerable citizens. Insurance has become a reality for crores of poor Indians. Unorganised sector workers have access to a pension for the first time. Long anguished farmers, falling into debt traps with each poor harvest, now find some succour through comprehensive crop insurance. Over 90 lakh farmers have benefited from the crop insurance scheme during the Kharif season last year and the Rabi season in 2016-17, claims of over ₹ 7,700 crore have already been paid to farmers under the Pradhan Mantri Fasal Bima Yojana.

CLAIMS UNDER PMJDY FOR LIFE COVER OF ₹30,000

(as on August 18, 2017)

Claims received	4,794
Claims paid	4201
Rejected claims	581
Claims in process	12

PROGRESS UNDER PRADHAN MANTRI JEEVAN JYOTI BIMA YOJANA

As on August 7, 2017

Gross enrolment reported by banks, subject to verification of eligibility, etc.	34,611,000
Total no. of claims received	73,584
Total no. of claims disbursed	68,681

Source: www.jansuraksha.gov.in

CLAIMS UNDER PMJDY FOR ACCIDENTAL INSURANCE COVER OF ₹1 LAKH

(As on August 18, '17)

Claims received	2,576
Claims paid	1,817
Claim processed (payment awaited)	26
Rejected claims	559
Claims in process	174

PROGRESS UNDER PRADHAN MANTRI SURAKSHA BIMA YOJANA

As on Aug 7, '17

Gross enrolment reported by banks, subject to verification of eligibility, etc.	109,550,000
Total no. of claims received	15,402
Total no. of claims disbursed	11,383

PROGRESS UNDER PRADHAN MANTRI MUDRA YOJANA

At FY17-end, ₹ cr

No of loan accounts	39,701,047
Loan amount sanctioned	180,529
Loan amount disbursed	175,312
Outstanding amount	138,209

Source: www.mudra.org.in

❖ Financial Inclusion

The Jan Dhan Yojana created 300 million new bank accounts. Despite naysayers, most new accounts remain active and have positive balances. Women, especially in rural India, can save and get more control over their finances and their lives. Bank accounts unlocked the power of direct benefit transfers; 200 million beneficiaries no longer need to stand in line or pay touts to get their own money. To ensure inclusive development, the government is promoting digital inclusion by providing mobile connectivity to over 55000 villages by March 2019 and initiating measures like Jandhan accounts debit cards, Aadhar Pay, Bharat Interface for Money (BHIM), to put an end to middlemen and ensure that benefits of various government schemes directly reach beneficiaries through digital transactions that touched 1569.3 crore in FY 17 till January. There is a target of 2500 crore digital transactions in 2017-18. This is a very significant scheme that strives to end Financial Untouchability by ensuring that the economically weaker sections have access to bank accounts.

❖ Rural Electrification

Pradhan Mantri Sahaj Bijli Har Ghar Yojana (Saubhagya scheme)

The scheme aims to provide 24X7 electricity to all the willing households. The Centre will be providing funds to states and union territories to undertake electrification of all areas. Families eligible for free electricity connection will be identified using Socio-Economic and Caste Census (SECC) 2011 data.

Under the Pradhan Mantri Sahaj Bijli Har Ghar Yojana (Saubhagya scheme), the Centre with the support of State Power Departments and discoms, has connected about 2.39 crore households since the launch of the scheme in September 2017. It is also expected to significantly improve the quality of life in underdeveloped regions alongwith encouraging the demand for bulbs and appliances. The International Energy Agency (IEA) recently said India's move to energise every village in the country with electricity was one of the greatest success stories in the world this year.

It aims to improve environment, public health, education and connectivity. The Saubhagya scheme will help India meet its global climate change commitments as electricity will substitute kerosene for lighting. It will also help improve education, health, and connectivity apart from having a multiplier effect on increased economic activities and job creation.

Entrepreneurship Opportunities

Start Up India provided the framework, and Mudra provided capital. Hundred million-plus Mudra loans suggest millions of entrepreneurial dreams becoming a reality. Equalising opportunity also meant incumbent "seths" lost the right to control businesses forever. The skill development programme, covering 45 lakh households, has been making a significant contribution to give a boost to Pradhan Mantri Mudra Yojana (PMMY). The success of this scheme, aimed at unorganised sector, can be gauged from the fact that in FY 18, a record ₹ 1.80 lakh crore of loans have been sanctioned, immensely benefiting entrepreneurs.

Clean India

Vast numbers of Indians live in squalor, often in close proximity to oases of privileged first world living. Swachh Bharat metamorphosed our approach to civic responsibility. Cleanliness is not the municipality's, the neighbour's or the sweeper's responsibility. It has become everyone's obligation. Initially derided by many elites, more than 70 million new toilets are testimony to a newfound self-esteem for millions of underprivileged — especially women and children in India's remotest corners. Similarly, the drive to make government buildings accessible to the disabled is a step towards making them full members of an inclusive India.

GST: Help for small businesses

The government, on January 10, announced a change in Goods and Services Tax (GST) rules that would exempt an additional 20 lakh small businesses. Businesses with annual sales of up to ₹ 40 lakh will be exempted from GST. Currently, firms with an annual turnover of up to ₹ 20 lakh are exempted. The changes will come into effect in April.

Mr. Jaitley announced that the limit for eligibility for the Composition Scheme would be raised to an annual turnover of ₹ 1.5 crore from April 1, 2019. He added that companies opting for the Composition Scheme would be allowed to file annual returns and pay taxes quarterly from April 1. Mr. Jaitley said that the Council had decided to extend the Composition Scheme to small service providers with an annual turnover of up to 50 lakh, at a tax rate of 6%.

The Confederation of All India Traders, in a statement, said that increasing the GST threshold limit would allow about 10 lakh traders to be exempted from the compliance burden of GST, and added that increasing the Composition Scheme limit would benefit about 20 lakh small businesses that fall between the annual turnover brackets of ₹ 1 crore and ₹ 1.5 crore.

Pradhan Mantri Awas Yojana

The Pradhan Mantri Awas Yojana (PMAY) has recently expanded its scope to cater to the housing needs of the mid-income group, besides the economically weaker sections (EWS) and low-income group (LIG). Early this month, the Prime Minister doubled the quantum of loan eligible for interest benefits under the PMAY in urban areas to 12 lakh.

PMAY scheme comprises of four key aspects. One, it aims to transform slum areas by building homes for slum dwellers in collaboration with private developers. Two, it plans to give a credit-linked subsidy to weaker and mid income sections on loans taken for new construction or renovation of existing homes.

Over 88,000 beneficiaries have been disbursed CLSS in Gujarat, while 74,000 people have availed the subsidy in Madhya Pradesh in three categories - economically weaker section (EWS), low income group (LIG) and middle income group (MIG) categories under the PMAY (U).

Pradhan Mantri Ujjwala Yojana

Modi Government launched Pradhan Mantri Ujjwala Yojana (PMUY) on 1st May, 2016 and it is implemented by Ministry of Petroleum and Natural Gas through its Oil Marketing Companies i.e., IOC, BPCL and HPCL through their network of distributors across the country. Through PMUY, initially, 5 crore BPL households were targeted for providing deposit free LPG connections to BPL households by 31st March, 2019. In a record time of 28 months for its launch, PMUY achieved the initial target of providing 5 crore LPG connection to BPL households. In the current year, considering the huge success of the Scheme, target was revised to 8 crores with budgetary allocation of ₹ 12,800 crore.

States of Uttar Pradesh (87 lakh), West Bengal (67 lakh), Bihar (61 lakh), Madhya Pradesh (45 lakh), Rajasthan (37 lakh) and Odisha (30 lakh) have accounted for nearly 65% of the connections provided. 47% of the beneficiaries are from the weaker sections of the society i.e., SC/STs.

PMUY aims at providing clean-cooking fuel to the poor households, which are otherwise vulnerable to various health hazards associated with indoor air pollution and bringing in qualitative changes in the living standards. Beneficiaries are identified through Socio-Economic Caste Census List-2011 and in such cases where names are not covered under SECC list, beneficiaries are identified from seven categories which includes SC/ST households, beneficiaries of PMAY(Gramin), Antyodaya Anna Yojana, Most Backward Classes, Forest Dwellers, Resident of Islands/River Islands and Tea Garden & Ex-tea Garden Tribes.

Pradhan Mantri Gram Sadak Yojana (PMGSY)

It is a one-time special intervention of the Union Government to provide rural connectivity, by way of single all-weather road, to the eligible unconnected habitations in the core network. Under PMGSY, all eligible unconnected habitations with more than 500 population in plain areas, 250+ population in Special Category States (Arunachal Pradesh, Assam, Manipur, Meghalaya, Mizoram, Nagaland, Sikkim, Tripura, Himachal Pradesh, Jammu and Kashmir and Uttarakhand), the Desert Areas (as identified in the District Development Programme), the Tribal (Schedule V) areas and Selected Tribal and Backward districts as identified by the Ministry of Home Affairs/NITI Aayog as per 2001 census are to be connected by all weather road. For critical Left Wing Extremism (LWE) affected blocks in nine States of Andhra Pradesh, Bihar, Chhattisgarh, Jharkhand, Madhya Pradesh, Maharashtra, Odisha, Uttar Pradesh and West Bengal (as identified by MHA), additional relaxation has been given to connect habitations with population of 100 persons and above.

Deen Dayal Upadhyaya Grameen Kaushalya Yojana (DDU-GKY) - Skill Development for Inclusive Growth

- Enable Poor and Marginalized to Access Benefits Demand led skill training at no cost to the rural poor
- Inclusive Program Design Mandatory coverage of socially disadvantaged groups (SC/ST 50%; Minority 15%; Women 33%
- Shifting Emphasis from Training to Career Progression

Stand-Up India

It is aimed at promoting entrepreneurship specifically among certain disadvantaged sections of society. It spans both the categories of 'inclusive growth' and 'building (income) security'. It is launched to boost the spirit of entrepreneurship among the most vulnerable groups of the society. The specific groups are scheduled caste, scheduled tribes and women. Under the umbrella of this scheme every single branch of a public sector bank is asked to support one entrepreneur each from women and SC/ST category. If implemented properly, the scheme, meant to promote entrepreneurship among Scheduled Castes/ Scheduled Tribes as well as women, has the potential to provide an alternative to traditional caste-based reservation in long run.

Ayushman Bharat

It is designed to not only make curative (hospital) care accessible to the poor through the National Health Protection Mission, but also to make promotive and preventive care available to all. Because of its promotive health components, it spans 'human development'.

Transparency in governance

The success of the government's drive to inclusion as could be deduced from the above testimonies also hinges on the government's push towards achieving greater transparency and stronger compliance with the government machinery. This is exemplified through the Direct Benefit Transfer scheme, aimed at transferring benefits directly to the recipients' bank accounts that was subsequently recognised as the world's largest cash transfer program.

Way Forward: for Inclusive Development

In four years, the Modi government has sought to "include" all Indians — rural, urban, differently enabled, young, old in a "new" Indian economic story but more steps are required to be taken. Some of them are:

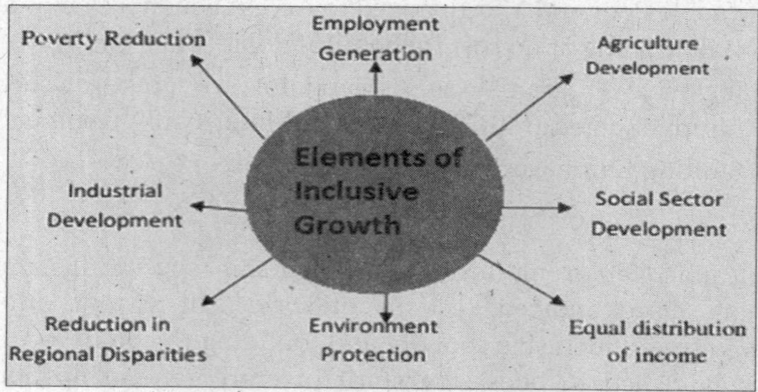

Improving the delivery of core public services

As incomes rise, citizens are demanding better delivery of core public services such as water and power supply, education, policing, sanitation, roads and public health. As physical access to services improves, issues of quality have become more central.

There are four avenues for reform: internal reform of public sector agencies; producing regular and reliable information for citizens; strengthening local governments and decentralizing responsibilities; and expanding the role of non-state providers.

Maintaining rapid growth while making growth more inclusive: With growing disparities between urban and rural areas, prosperous and lagging states, skilled and low-skilled workers, the primary medium term policy challenge for India is not to raise growth from 8 to 10 percent but to sustain rapid growth while spreading its benefits more widely.

Labor regulations: India's restrictive labor regulations have constrained the growth of the formal manufacturing sector. Better designed regulations can attract more labor- intensive investment and improve the job prospects for India's unemployed millions, those trapped in poor quality jobs, and the 80 million new entrants who are expected to join the work force over the next decade.

Financial sector: Problems in accessing finance are a major impediment to the performance of small and medium sized businesses in India. Improving financial intermediation and ensuring broader access to financial services is critical for equalizing growth. Inclusive growth needs financial institutions to be strong and efficient.

Agriculture and the Rural Economy

Raising agricultural productivity requires a return to investments in agricultural technology and infrastructure. Getting the rural economy moving will also require facilitating rural-nonfarm entrepreneurship.

Lagging States

Faster economic growth has seen rising inter-state disparities. Lagging states need to bring more jobs to their people by creating an attractive investment destination.

Reforming cumbersome regulatory procedures, improving rural connectivity, establishing law and order, creating a stable platform for natural resource investment that balances business interests with social concerns, and providing rural finance are important. Good understanding and coordination between the government machinery is essential for development and inclusive growth.

Right To Information Act

This Act will spread awareness among the people about different schemes introduced by the government from time to time and their implementation. This will help them for better utilization of the schemes.

Public-Private Partnerships

Public-private partnerships (PPP) can play a primary role in the provision of services of all types, from telecommunications to health, from airport modernization to primary education.

Social Development

In the social sector, significant achievements in education and health have taken place. India belongs to the Medium Human Development category. UNDP 2018 report says that Indian income has grown, but development has not taken place. It also pointed out that the income inequality is increasing. Social indicators are much lower for Scheduled castes and Scheduled tribes. Malnutrition among children is one major problem, 46% of children suffer from malnutrition. All the aspects mentioned above should be given top priority for enabling inclusive growth.

Empowerment and Opportunity

In order to achieve inclusive growth, policy reforms should focus on empowerment and opportunity—enabling all Indian citizens to engage with the emerging economy on fair terms. Though expanding rural infrastructure is important, but without complementary investments in empowerment, opportunity will not be enough. Increased access to rural finance is important, but only if embedded with other reforms to make the rural economy work for the poor.

Accountability of Reforms

Outlays do not necessarily mean outcomes. The people of country are concerned with outcomes only. However, emphasis should be laid on the need to improve the quality of implementation and enhance the efficiency and accountability of the delivery mechanism. The fruits of reforms are now being enjoyed by the rich and to some extent by the middle class but these are not reaching the poor. Hence, efforts should be made in this direction.

Inclusive Growth with Respect to Employment:

Generation of productive employment (decent work) for labour force in the economy, as employment is a key to inclusive growth

Employment generation in all sectors, regions and for all socio-economic groups.

Particularly for poorer sections of population, backward regions, lagging sectors and ST / SC / OBC / women etc.

❖ LAND

While raising agricultural productivity is a must to cope issue with the shrinkage of agricultural land, the very slow growth of non-farm opportunities for employment (the rising demand for industrialization, including SEZs, and for housing in expanding urban areas) and livelihoods and social security for small holders poses a challenge and argue for a careful and calibrated approach for land acquisition.

Inclusive Governance

Governance has to be viewed and shaped in the context of ongoing social change through the functioning of our democratic system. Experience has amply demonstrated that anticipatory or inclusive governance is indispensable for achieving inclusive growth.

Conclusion

With several policy endeavours like PM Awas Yojana that aims to end India's homelessness completely, labour reforms under the principle of 'Shrameva Jayate, Mudra Yojana which aims to create sustainable livelihood opportunities, Swachh Bharat Mission that aims for a clean and healthy India, Ujjwala Yojana that enables a smoke-free cooking environment for women with free LPG connections, creating village level entrepreneurs by setting up Common Service Centres under the Digital India Program, connecting rural habitations under the Digital India program, connecting parts of rural India under the PM Sadak Yojana and many others are initiatives designed with an aim to promote an inclusive and sustainable development of the society.

In conclusion one could aptly concede that both at the policy level and in terms of implementation, the government led by PM Narendra Modi has ensured the trickling down effect of the government schemes true to its mandate of "Sabka saath, sabka vikas' (inclusive development).

❑❑❑

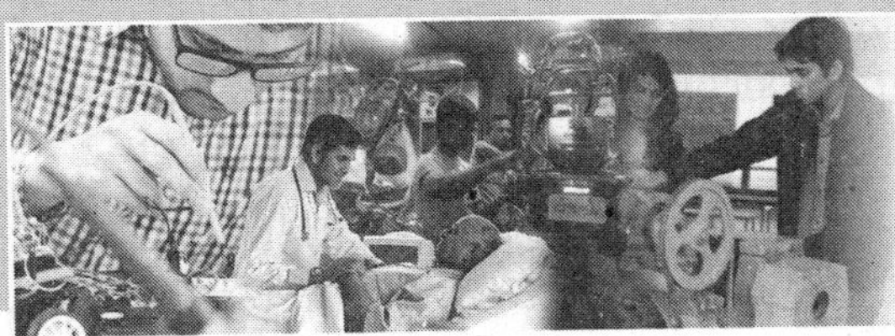

Chapter 12

Entrepreneurship Education and Skilling Entrepreneurs

Skilling and Entrepreneurship complete each other. Skills are fundamental, but not sufficient for gaining decent jobs. Improved productivity through skill development must be complemented by economic growth and employment opportunities. They are, collectively, a prerequisite to the Government's pursuit of holistic development of the nation. Entrepreneurship education and skilling Entrepreneurs will ensure sufficient employment opportunities for the skilled workforce. Unleashed entrepreneurship, besides employment generation, will also utilize the youth power for productivity improvement and wealth creation; thus, stimulating equitable development and a sustainable path for decent livelihood creation for the country. Technology and resources have to be judiciously harnessed to achieve the same. Furthermore, endeavors need to be aligned to ensure the outreach of opportunities and services to the bottom of the economic pyramid, facilitated by enterprises.

What is Entrepreneurship Education?

Entrepreneurship education is about transforming an idea into reality and then actually trying to do it. It is opposite to the academic approach where you only talk about entrepreneurship and study books.Entrepreneurship education is a practical task where you design your education in such a way that you make the students "do it". A lecturer must push the students to act and try some of the startup activities in real life situations.For instance, making the students go to the surrounding area of the school and talk to businesses and shopkeepers, find possible customers and ask their opinion on the product or service they are planning to sell. Then the teachers can dicuss with the students the findings from the real world experience.

Importance of Entrepreneurship Education

Entrepreneurship education has the mandate to equip the youth with functional knowledge and skill to build up their character, attitude and vision. It has vital role in developing eco-system that promotes innovation (European Union, 2006).EU remarks its importance for providing the base for innovation and creating a value system; and developing entrepreneurial culture, which drives wealth creation and gives further push to innovations.

Skilling Entrepreneurs

Entrepreneurial skills centre around attitudes (soft skills), such as persistence, networking and self-confidence on the one hand and enabling skills (hard skills) on the other hand, including basic start- up knowledge, business planning, financial literacy and managerial skills. Effective entrepreneurship education policies and programmes focus on developing these entrepreneurial competencies and skills, which are transferable and beneficial in many work contexts. The aim is not only to strengthen the capacity and desire of more individuals to start their own enterprises, but also to develop an entrepreneurial culture in society.

Entrepreneurship Needs More

Knowledge is power, to the greatest extent yet correct utilization of that knowledge is what is required. Bookish knowledge provides a solid platform but one has to transcend beyond that, to be considered as a lion amongst meerkats. For that, one needs to realize his/her potential and channelize it in the right direction. The ability to critically gauge the situation and come up with the best possible solution, in tandem to the working ethics of his employees and co-workers, is the hallmark of an adept entrepreneur- something that can be harnessed through critical life-skills.

Situation in India

Over the last few years, entrepreneurship has emerged as a sustained medium of education for employment opportunities across the world. However, entrepreneurship education in India is still at its nascent stage.

Several actions have been taken by the Indian government to bring out the relationship between education and entrepreneurship. For example, the Indian government's Start-up India Campaign focuses on job creation.

Recently, the government of Kerala announced that it will grant a one-year break from regular studies to the engineering students who aspire to take up the path of entrepreneurship and build their own companies. When their break ends, these students will be allowed to return and continue with their engineering studies.

On similar lines, prestigious engineering as well as management institutes of India including IIT-Mumbai and Kanpur, IIM-Udaipur, have introduced 'deferred placements' for their students.

All these initiatives by colleges, supported by Government of India, are aimed at promoting entrepreneurship among students. A number of efforts like these which encourage 'The Spirit of Entrepreneurship' are being initiated by colleges one after the other. After all, Entrepreneurship is greatest asset for any nation's economy.Services, wealth, jobs, facilities etc. are all created by these entrepreneurial individuals.

A few of India's efforts at promoting entrepreneurship and innovation are:

Startup India: Through the Startup India initiative, Government of India promotes entrepreneurship by mentoring, nurturing and facilitating startups throughout their life cycle. Since its launch in January 2016, the initiative has successfully given a head start to numerous aspiring entrepreneurs. With a

360 degree approach to enable startups, the initiative provides a comprehensive four-week free online learning program, has set up research parks, incubators and startup centres across the country by creating a strong network of academia and industry bodies. More importantly, a 'Fund of Funds' has been created to help startups gain access to funding. At the core of the initiative is the effort to build an ecosystem in which startups can innovate and excel without any barriers, through such mechanisms as online recognition of startups, Startup India Learning Programme, Facilitated Patent filing, Easy Compliance Norms, Relaxed Procurement Norms, incubator support, innovation focused programmes for students, funding support, tax benefits and addressing of regulatory issues.

Make in India: Designed to transform India into a global design and manufacturing hub, the Make in India initiative was launched in September 2014. It came as a powerful call to India's citizens and business leaders, and an invitation to potential partners and investors around the world to overhaul out-dated processes and policies, and centralize information about opportunities in India's manufacturing sector. This has led to renewed confidence in India's capabilities among potential partners abroad, business community within the country and citizens at large. The plan behind Make in India was one of the largest undertaken in recent history. Among several other measures, the initiative has ensured the replacement of obsolete and obstructive frameworks with transparent and user-friendly systems. This has in turn helped procure investments, foster innovation, develop skills, protect intellectual property and build best-in-class manufacturing infrastructure.

Atal Innovation Mission (AIM): AIM is the Government of India's endeavour to promote a culture of innovation and entrepreneurship, and it serves as a platform for promotion of world-class Innovation Hubs, Grand Challenges, start-up businesses and other self-employment activities, particularly in technology driven areas. In order to foster curiosity, creativity and imagination right at the school, AIM recently launched Atal Tinkering Labs (ATL) across India. ATLs are workspaces where students can work with tools and equipment to gain hands-on training in the concepts of STEM (Science, Technology,

Engineering and Math). Atal Incubation Centres (AICs) are another programme of AIM created to build innovative start-up businesses as scalable and sustainable enterprises. AICs provide world class incubation facilities with appropriate physical infrastructure in terms of capital equipment and operating facilities. These incubation centres, with a presence across India, provide access to sectoral experts, business planning support, seed capital, industry partners and training to encourage innovative start-ups.

Support to Training and Employment Programme for Women (STEP): STEP was launched by the Government of India's Ministry of Women and Child Development to train women with no access to formal skill training facilities, especially in rural India. The Ministry of Skill Development & Entrepreneurship and NITI Aayog recently redrafted the Guidelines of the 30-year-old initiative to adapt to present-day needs. The initiative reaches out to all Indian women above 16 years of age. The programme imparts skills in several sectors such as agriculture, horticulture, food processing, handlooms, traditional crafts like embroidery, travel and tourism, hospitality, computer and IT services.

Jan Dhan- Aadhaar- Mobile (JAM): JAM, for the first time, is a technological intervention that enables direct transfer of subsidies to intended beneficiaries and, therefore, eliminates all intermediaries and leakages in the system, which has a potential impact on the lives of millions of Indian citizens. Besides serving as a vital check on corruption, JAM provides for accounts to all underserved regions, in order to make banking services accessible down to the last mile.

Digital India: The Digital India initiative was launched to modernize the Indian economy by making all government services available in a digital form. The initiative aims to transform India into a digitally-empowered society and knowledge economy with universal access to goods and services. Given historically poor internet penetration, this initiative aims to make available high-speed internet down to the grassroots. This program aims to improve citizen participation in the digital and financial space, make India's cyberspace safer and more secure, and improve ease of doing business. Digital India hopes to achieve equity and efficiency in a country with immense diversity by making digital resources and services available in all Indian languages.

Biotechnology Industry Research Assistance Council (BIRAC): BIRAC is a not-for-profit Public-Sector Enterprise, set up by Department of Biotechnology to strengthen and empower emerging biotechnology enterprises. It aims to embed strategic research and innovation in all biotech enterprises, and bridge the existing gaps between industry and academia. The ultimate goal is to develop high-quality, yet affordable products with the use of cutting edge technologies. BIRAC has initiated partnerships with several national and global partners for building capacities of the Indian biotech industry, particularly start-ups and SME's, and has facilitated several rapid developments in medical technology.

Department of Science and Technology (DST): The DST comprises several arms that work across the spectrum on all major projects that require scientific and technological intervention. The Technology Interventions for Disabled and Elderly, for instance, provides technological solutions to address challenges and improve quality of life of the elderly in India through the application of science and technology. On the other hand, the ASEAN-India Science, Technology and Innovation Cooperation works to narrow the development gap and enhance connectivity between the ASEAN countries. It encourages cooperation in science, technology and innovation through joint research across sectors and provides fellowships to scientists and researchers from ASEAN member states with Indian R&D/ academic institutions to upgrade their research skills and expertise.

Stand-Up India: Launched in 2015, Stand-Up India seeks to leverage institutional credit for the benefit of India's underprivileged. It aims to enable economic participation of, and share the benefits of India's growth, among women entrepreneurs, Scheduled Castes and Scheduled Tribes. Towards this end, at least one women and one individual from the SC or ST communities are granted loans between ₹ 1 million to ₹ 10 million to set up greenfield enterprises in manufacturing, services or the trading sector. The Stand-Up India portal also acts as a digital platform for small entrepreneurs and provides information on financing and credit guarantee.

Trade Related Entrepreneurship Assistance and Development (TREAD): To address the critical issues of access to credit among India's underprivileged women, the TREAD programme enables credit availability to interested women through non-governmental organizations (NGOs). As such, women can receive support of registered NGOs in both accessing loan facilities, and receiving counselling and training opportunities to kick-start proposed enterprises, in order to provide pathways for women to take up non-farm activities.

Pradhan Mantri Kaushal Vikas Yojana (PMKVY): A flagship initiative of the Ministry of Skill Development & Entrepreneurship (MSDE), this is a Skill Certification initiative that aims to train youth in industry-relevant skills to enhance opportunities for livelihood creation and employability. Individuals with prior learning experience or skills are also assessed and certified as a Recognition of Prior Learning. Training and Assessment fees are entirely borne by the Government under this program.

National Skill Development Mission: Launched in July 2015, the mission aims to build synergies across sectors and States in skilled industries and initiatives. With a vision to build a 'Skilled India' it is designed to expedite decision-making across sectors to provide skills at scale, without compromising on quality or speed. The seven sub-missions proposed in the initial phase to guide the mission's skilling efforts across India are: (i) Institutional Training, (ii) Infrastructure, (iii) Convergence, (iv) Trainers, (v) Overseas Employment, (vi) Sustainable Livelihoods and (vii) Leveraging Public Infrastructure.

Science for Equity Empowerment and Development (SEED): SEED aims to provide opportunities to motivated scientists and field level workers to undertake action-oriented, location specific projects for socio-economic gain, particularly in rural areas. Efforts have been made to associate national labs and other specialist S&T institutions with innovations at the grassroots to enable access to inputs from experts, quality infrastructure. SEED emphasizes equity in development, so that the benefits of technological accrue to a vast section of the population, particularly the disadvantaged.

Way Forward: Recommended Actions

Embed entrepreneurship in formal and informal education

- Mainstream the development of entrepreneurship awareness and entrepreneurial behaviours starting from primary school level (e.g., risk taking, teamwork behaviours, etc.)

- Promote entrepreneurship through electives, extracurricular activities, career awareness seminars and visits to businesses at secondary school level
- Support entrepreneurship courses, programmes and chairs at higher educational institutions and universities
- Promote vocational training and apprenticeship programmes
- Promote and link up with entrepreneurship training centres

Develop effective entrepreneurship curricula

- Prepare basic entrepreneurial skills education material
- Encourage tailored local material, case studies and role models
- Foster interactive and on-line tools
- Promote experiential and learning- by- doing methodologies

Train teachers

- Ensure teachers engage with the private sector and with entrepreneurs and support initiatives that bring entrepreneurs to educational establishments
- Encourage entrepreneurship training for teachers
- Promote entrepreneurship educators' networks

Strengthen the institutional framework

- Designate a lead institution
- Set up an effective coordination mechanism and clarify mandates
- Engage with the private sector and other stakeholders
- Ensure business-like service delivery

Partner with the private sector

- Encourage private sector sponsorship for entrepreneurship training and skill development
- Link up business with entrepreneurship education networks
- Develop mentoring programmes

Conclusion

The Government of India has undertaken several initiatives and instituted policy measures to foster a culture of innovation and entrepreneurship in the country. Job creation is the foremost challenge faced by India. With a significant and unique demographic advantage; India, however, has immense potential to innovate, raise entrepreneurs and create jobs for the benefit of the nation and the world.

In the recent years, a wide spectrum of new programmes and opportunities to nurture innovation has been created by the Government of India across a number of sectors. From engaging with academia, industry, investors, small and big entrepreneurs, non-governmental organizations to the most underserved sections of society.

Recognising the importance of women entrepreneurship and economic participation in enabling the country's growth and prosperity, Government of India has ensured that all policy initiatives are geared towards enabling equal opportunity for women. The government seeks to bring women to the forefront of India's entrepreneurial ecosystem by providing access to loans, networks, markets and training.

❑❑❑

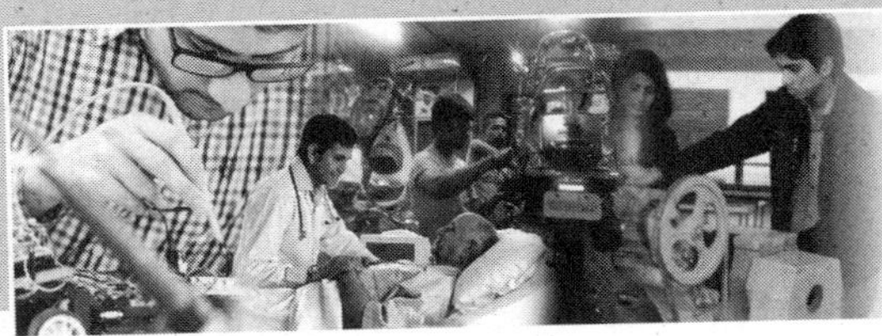

Chapter 13

Conclusion and Recommendation

Education is considered the most powerful tool for bringing in social and economic change. A well-educated group of people is sufficiently equipped with knowledge and skill which is not only important to assist economic growth, but is also a prerequisite to ensure inclusive growth as it is the educated and skilled people who derive the maximum benefit from the employment opportunities which growth tends to offer.

Skills and knowledge are powerful components to ensure economic progress and social development in any country. Countries that have higher and better levels of skills make necessary adjustments more efficiently to meet the challenges and opportunities of the world of work. As India is progressively moving in the direction of becoming a 'knowledge economy', it becomes more and more significant that the country stresses on promotion of skills and these skills should have relevance for the progressive economic environment.

India is among the few countries in the world where the working age population will be more than those dependent on them and according to the World Bank, this is going to follow the same suit for a minimum of three decades till the end of 2040. This has more and more been identified as a potential strength for the economy of the country, provided we are in a position to equip and constantly improve the skills of people in the working age group. If India aims to grow into a manufacturing hub, given its need for generation of employment to garner the demographic advantage, it will have to give more emphasis on skill development as against the existing education system. Since education system of India has been distorted in favour of formal education with its more emphasis on academics, it has performed well in services/tertiary sector, as this sector is the most important beneficiary of formally educated workforce. However, manufacturing processes do not require academic skills to that extent, for most of the workforce. Consequently, the people who are employed in this sector may be uneducated or unskilled as low-end firms cannot manage to have college graduates; or they may be over-educated and yet unskilled for the desired tasks, even if some firms get ready to make the expected payment. The education that is needed for manufacturing is very basic in nature. This may just require a person to read and understand instructions and based on that make very basic judgements or estimations; however the skills actually required may vary from painting, welding, polishing, assembling, packaging, to handling equipment among many others. Thus, a comprehensive rebuilding of the present education system is the need of the hour. Taking note of these requirements, the Government of India has adopted skill development as a priority for the country over the coming 10 years of time. The Eleventh Five Year Plan comprises of a road map for the development of skills in India, and supported the constitution of Skill Development Missions, both at the level of State and country. For the creation of such an institutional base for the development of skill in India at the national level, a 'Coordinated Action on Skill Development' with a three-tier institutional structure comprising of the PM's National Council on Skill Development, the National Skill Development Coordination Board (NSDCB) and NSDC was constituted in early part of the year 2008.

The primary functions of the PM's National Council for developing Skills in India are as follows:

- To prepare a design of overall broad policy objectives, financing, and governance models and strategies associated with skill development.

- To examine the progress of schemes and provide necessary guidance on mid-course corrections, additions, or closing of parts or whole of any specific plan/programme/scheme.
- Coordinate Initiatives of Public/Private Sector in a scheme of synergistic action.

The NSDCB coordinates the skill development initiatives of a large number of Central Ministries/Departments and States. NSDC is a Public–Private Partnership, established to mobilize the establishment of large scale, long-lasting profit making vocational institutions in the country, through private sector participation and low-cost funding for training capacity. Besides, it is expected to fund supporting systems for quality assurance, labour market information systems and train-the-trainer facilities. Thus, the three-tier structure together helps to implement skill development on the ground by means of three main channels such as central ministries, the state governments, and private and public training organizations.

In the Central Government, about 20 Ministries have been involved in close monitoring of skill development. These ministries are functional in one of two ways—by building own training capacity in particular areas (instances of such ministries are MoLE, Ministry of Agriculture and Ministry of Health and Family Welfare and so on) or by offering per-trainee expense of training for specifically targeted populations (instances of such ministries comprise of MoRD, Ministry of Women and Child Development and so on).

Most of the State Governments have also constituted State Skill Development Missions that take the shape of nodal bodies for supporting the skill development programme in the State. SSDMs are believed to contribute significantly in improving the speed of skilling, by identifying important areas for skill development in the State, as along with coordinating with Central Ministries and State Line Departments, and industry or private training organizations. Each State follows a framework of SSDM that best suits the local needs and the vision for development of skills in the state. Though some States have decided to constitute the SSDM and consider it as a Society or Corporation under the Chief Secretary or Chief Minister, many other states have formed it under related Departments of Labour, Human Resource Development or Planning. Many states are beginning to create annual targets for skill development, with specific budgetary allocation of the state and supporting Government initiatives by encouraging private investment.

The Government has taken initiatives to launch a national Multi-Skill programme with the name Skill India. This programme aims to impart skills to the youth with a focus on employability and entrepreneur skills. It will also create training and support system for conventional professions such as welders, carpenters, cobblers, masons, blacksmiths, tailoring, nursing, weavers and so on. India is in dire need of skilled workforce in different areas such as construction, real estate, textile, transportation, jewellery designing, gem industry, tourism, banking along with many other sectors. Skill development infuses confidence, provides right direction and boosts productivity. Grooming of youth is necessary for blue-collar jobs and therefore, various schemes must be converged to achieve this objective, which is undoubtedly the need of the country. Government, Academia, corporate educational institutions, Non-Government Organizations and society, all should try making the skill development initiative the main focus for the economy to progress. The development of skill at early stages among youth, as early as school level is the need of the hour for ensuring suitable job opportunities. The training should be provided so that the youth could be skilled enough to find suitable jobs in any part of the world. Today the world should give equal importance to all jobs so as to ensure a balanced growth in all the sectors. Every person looking for job whether it is white collar or blue collar should be provided training in soft skills. Soft skills are required in every sector. Grooming, etiquette, hygiene, time management, safety, tolerance levels are needed to lead a desired and decent life. Skill development and the above mentioned grooming areas will have to reach the rural and remote areas. This will promote sophistication and infuse the much desired confidence among the youth. All this will assist individuals to take care of himself or herself along with his/her job most efficiently.

Major problems and reforms required in skill development can be summed up as follows:

In Education System: The present system of education does not give emphasis on training youth in employable skills so that they could get the most suitable employment opportunities. Today, a large portion of India's labour force has outdated skills. Keeping in mind the current and expected economic growth, this challenge will become more prominent in future, because more than 75 per cent of new job opportunities are believed to be 'skill-based'. Foundation for creating an efficient education delivery model includes the following:

Availability: An annual capacity of more than four million is required to be upgraded substantially so as to achieve the targeted skill requirements by the end of 2022. Today, a significant mismatch exists between the large population of unemployed youth and existing vacancies. This causes low employability quotient of people. Hence, it is most needed that the needs of both learners and the labour market are given more emphasis so as to make the required skills available through collaborations between public administrators, suppliers of educational services, industry and civil society. The availability of both physical infrastructure and human resource (teachers) with an aim to introduce skill-based training is the basic need of a learner, which should be addressed effectively.

Accessibility: The accessibility of skill-based training sees a big challenge because of India's large geographical area, challenging landscape and diverse social economic conditions. Some states have restricted access to such training. Consequently, the population consists of a huge unskilled workforce. Significant disparities are visible across states so far as socio-economic factors like education levels, income levels, industrial growth, etc., are concerned. A large portion of the population below the poverty line does not even have basic amenities, leave aside education and training. It is important to focus on the informal sector, which targets the people and institutions, thus promoting livelihood.

Adaptability: The growth of economy over the years has underlined the defects of skill development processes. Learners need a support system for national vocational qualification offering vertical mobility for those pursuing skills. This will enable learners to switch from skill-based training to academics and vice versa. They are in need of a support system for clear vocational qualification for establishing competency standards, affiliation and accreditation. The required system will merge skill training with academic standards. A more formalized system for vocational training will go a long way evoking greater reputation and acceptability for this initiative among youth and society at large.

Acceptability: The programs associated with skill development being imparted to learners should try achieving the most important quality of infrastructure (ICT and physical infrastructure), pedagogy and skill delivery methods.

The existing system of education does not train young people in employable skills who are always on a look out for employment opportunities. Keeping in mind the current and expected economic growth, this problem is believed to worsen as more than 75 per cent of the new job opportunities are going to be skill-based. This leads to a need to introduce an advanced curriculum framework that is based on industry's best practices. It is equally important to apply these forthcoming and extensively used learning methods to formulate skill development programs with an aim to train learners with something that is relevant and not obsolete.

In Industry Sector: Many establishments offer on-job training to their employees. This may acquire different forms: first, the workers may take training in an establishment under the guidance of a skilled supervisor; second, the workers may be offered off-campus training. In both these situations, establishments incur some expenses. Firms will, thus, emphasize the workers to work for a minimum-specific time period, after the completion of their on-the-job training, during which the firm believes to recover the benefits of the improved productivity because of training. But the retention ratio is always seen to be low, thus there is a lack of private and Industry Participation in ensuring skill development. No incentives are offered to private players so that they could enter the field of vocational education. Existing related regulations are not flexible. In-service training is needed but its prevalence is not seen today. Today, there is a lack of opportunity to ensure continuous skill upgradation. Moreover, the number of experienced and qualified teachers is also less who could train students on vocational skills.

Low Level of Participation by Women: Participation of women in vocational education and training is particularly low as against men. A few reasons in the form of social and cultural norms and family responsibilities are prevalent in our society that comes in the way of participation of women in vocational education or training. Women are also likely to get disheartened because of such family and social pressures, particularly in rural areas of the country. Hence, in order to raise enrolments, the joint initiatives with local NGOs and Panchayats should be taken up in order to inform women and their families on the benefits of vocational education, which may lead to their employability. Particularly, women should be explained as how to inculcate income-generating skills and activities within them so that they could ensure an improvement in their social and economic status.

Thus, a concerted effort in a number of important areas is needed to ensure the formation of skills in a demand driven manner. Reorientation of curriculum for skill development on a continuing basis is required to match the demands of the employers/industry and make it in agreement with the available self-employment opportunities. Improvement in accreditation and certification system is equally important. Establishing an institutional mechanism is also required to provide access to information on skill inventory and skill maps on a real time basis. For this, a sectoral-approach is required with special stress on those sectors with enhanced employment potential. Standards may be established by the industry-led sector skill councils, which should be made efficient in the Twelfth Plan, while the accreditation of certification processes should be achieved by independent, specialized agencies whose certification should be left totally to the institutions. An effort should be made towards establishing Skill Development Centres in existing education and training institutions. This will save a huge money and time. For skill development, a system of funding poor people through direct financial aid or loan can also be put in place. Apprenticeship training can be used as another mode for on-job training, which has to be re-modelled with an aim to be up-scaled significantly to make it more efficient.

Finally, vocational education at school level and vocational training through Industrial Training Institutes (ITIs) and Industrial Training Centres (ITCs) need expansion and drastic change. An urgent need to revisit the scheme for upgradation of governments ITIs as Centres of Excellence through the PPP has to be achieved to make them more efficient during the Twelfth Plan. Establishing flexible learning pathways integrated with schooling on one hand and higher education on the other through National Vocational Education Qualification Framework (NVEQF) is the need of the day. Promotion of Public-Private Partnerships in financing, service delivery, and provision of workspaces and training of trainers is equally important. Repositioning of employment exchanges as outreach points is required to be achieved. Removal of entry-barriers to private participation is very necessary while putting an effective regulatory framework for coordinating the network of Private players, along with supervising, evaluating and analysing results of different programmes. All of these issues have undergone thorough consideration during the Eleventh Plan; now operational details have to be planned and specific initiatives to be started during the implementation of Twelfth Plan.

The task of skill development comprises of a number of challenges in India, which include:

- Enhancing capacity and capability of present system for ensuring equitable access to all.
- Promoting learning for whole life, retaining quality and relevance, as per the changing needs, particularly of growing knowledge economy.
- Developing potent convergence between school education, various skill development efforts of government and between government and Private Sector initiatives.
- Capacity building of institutions for planning, assurance of quality and participation of stakeholders.
- Building institutional mechanism for development of research, assuring quality, examinations and certification, affiliations and accreditation.
- Enhancing participation of stakeholders, mobilizing sufficient investment for funding skill development,

achieving sustainability by strengthening physical and intellectual resources.

Despite increasing productivity and rising education levels, India is still in need of improving its educational achievements. It has huge deficits on vital quantitative education indicators (average years of education and net secondary enrolments) and demand for workers having technical/vocational skills seems to be on decline. Besides, very little is known about qualitative indicators–as India does not seem to take part in standardized international examinations and good comparative measures of quality are lacking. The relative shortage in the number of educated workers in India shows inadequate investment in education in the past. However, any shortage in the future flow of educated entrants to the labour market has to be lessened. However, the demand for educated/skilled workers in India is on the rise. For maintaining high productivity levels and competing efficiently with rapidly growing economies, India will have to formulate policies so as to ensure that more people obtain higher quality education and more skills.

India has been one of the most populous countries of the world with its population being 1.32 billion. News reports say that in just another decade, about 70 per cent of its population is likely to lie in the working age group. Such a large working population will definitely put pressure on the government to have high priority for generation of employment and elimination of poverty for its people. Today, we are still grappling with the problem of universal education. We also need to take into account the drop out of more than 5 million children from our education system on annual basis. Despite our efforts to make education accessible to large numbers, employability of the youth is one of the biggest problems that require urgent attention. Only about 5 per cent of the whole workforce present in the country may be considered to have had access to some form of formal skills training. The dream to transform India into the world's favourite destination seems to be stumbling when a high proportion of trained workforce is available in other countries. According to some studies, about 68 per cent of the workforce is trained in the UK, in Germany this figure is about 75 per cent and in the USA, it is 52 percent. Talking of Asia, 80 per cent of the Japanese workforce is immensely trained and skilled while in South Korea, this is as high as 96 per cent.

In the June month of 2016, the government of India introduced sweeping changes to the FDI (Foreign Direct Investment) policy of the country. Such radical liberalization refers to a number of important sectors ranging from civil aviation, defence, pharmaceuticals and single brand retail are now open to 100 per cent foreign ownership. Since 2002, for the first time India has got featured among the top 10 FDI attracting countries of the world. Does our skills development programme support our ambitions? As per the recent estimates, about 104 million young men and women in the country are likely to be in need of skills training in the coming 6 years. During the same time period, some 298 million people (part of the current workforce) will also be up for retraining or for updating their skillsets with newer learning. It is right time India takes skills development with all seriousness since this is going to lay the foundation of economic development of the nation.

The NDA government has very rightly recognized the need for training and skills development in the country. The initiation of the PMKVY in the month of July in 2015, under the aegis of NSDC, was a first step in this direction. The scheme was started on 15 July 2015, a day described as National Skills Day to underline the significance of the PMKVY. The initial target of the initiative is to train about 2.4 million youth from the lower income strata of Indian society. The outlay planned for the PMKVY is approximately INR 1,500 crore. The government has collaborated with many training facilities across the country to create about 2,300 training centres for imparting different skills based training. Training, examination, and certification are one side of the programme and promoting entrepreneurial ambitions is another. The PMKVY ultimately aims to fit India with the skill requirements that are being searched by investors.

Collaborating with the Private Sector: The great task of skills development in India and transforming the nation into the skills capital of the world is not something to be achieved by the government alone. No matter how big the budgetary allocation, unless the government takes steps to rope in the private sector, neither the programme is going to be sustainable, nor will it be in a position to enhance employment opportunities for the youth. A number of such joint cooperative training programmes with private companies have witnessed great success. Bosch, the German engineering and electronics manufacturer, for instance has been one of the best collaborators when it comes to training the Indian youth from their centres in Bengaluru.

Skills Development for Social Empowerment: The big challenge of employability of youth is the one the government is trying to address by providing skill based training and by initiating many other skill development programs. This may also be important for uplifting a great number of families from below poverty line. Despite its immense contribution in building the nation and restructuring economy of the country, it is worth noting that the government start expanding the scope and focus on PMKVY. Connecting the Skill India program with central and state government recruitment mechanisms is equally vital.

It is easy to dream of an ambitious task. It is quite certain that we are all aspiring for a glorious India to ride the momentum of development and transform itself into the go-to destination when we talk of manufacturing and services. But practically speaking, we need to bridge a huge gap before we come close to fulfil this ambition. Empowerment of the youth and creating a self-reliant generation must in fact begin with equipping the youth with skills, which in turn will allow them to work and evolve themselves in the years to come.

❑❑❑

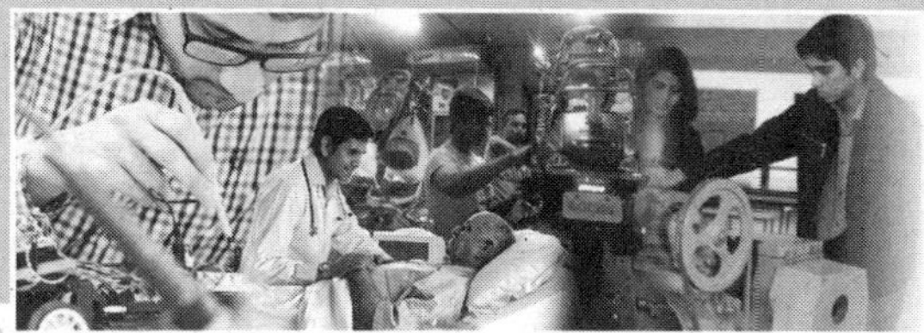

Glossary of Terms

Aadhaar

Aadhaar is a 12-digit unique identification number issued by the Indian government to every individual resident of India. The Unique Identification Authority of India (UDAI), which functions under the Planning Commission of India, is responsible for managing Aadhaar numbers and Aadhaar identification cards.

❖ Aadhaar ID in North-East Region

Aadhaar IDs are not available in some of the states in the North-East Region. To facilitate coverage of those states in PMKVY, alternate Identity proofs, such as PAN or Voter ID, may be accepted instead of the Aadhaar ID. The six North-East states where alternate IDs can be used are Nagaland, Manipur, Mizoram, Arunachal Pradesh, Assam and Meghalaya. Variation from the process shall not be permitted for the remaining North-East States, namely Sikkim and Tripura.

❖ Accreditation (of programmes, institutions)

The process of accrediting an institution of education or training, a programme of study, or a service, showing it has been approved by the relevant legislative and professional authorities by having met predetermined standards.

❖ **Activities (professional)**

A set of tasks corresponding to functions required for the delivery of goods and services in an enterprise belonging to a specific sector.

❖ **Assessment**

The sum of methods and processes used to evaluate the attainments (knowledge, know-how, skills and competences) of an individual, and typically leading to certification.

❖ **Awarding body**

A body issuing qualifications (certificates or diplomas) formally recognizing the achievements of an individual, following a standard assessment procedure.

❖ **Basic skills (key competences)**

The skills and competences needed to function in contemporary society, e.g. listening, speaking, reading, writing and mathematics.

❖ **Certificate/diploma**

An official document, issued by an awarding body, which records the achievements of an individual following a standard assessment procedure.

❖ **Certification (of knowledge, skills and competences)**

The process of formally validating knowledge, know-how and/or skills and competences acquired by an individual, following a standard assessment procedure. Certificates or diplomas are issued by accredited awarding bodies.

❖ **Cluster**

Geographical unit where a concentration of more or less interconnected enterprises of the same sector can be found, as well as various training providers in the same sector.

❖ **Comparability of qualifications**

The extent to which it is possible to establish equivalence between the level and content of formal qualifications (certificates or diplomas) at sectoral, regional, national or international levels.

❖ **Competence**

Ability to apply knowledge, know-how and skills in a habitual and/or changing work situation.

❖ **Credit points (or credits)**

Credit points are allocated to qualifications and to the units that constitute them. By agreement, they represent, in numerical form the volume of learning outcomes, the relative importance of each of the units that make up a qualification, in relation to the expected results, i.e. the knowledge, skills and competences that must be acquired and assessed, regardless of the learning pathway.

❖ **Credit system**

A system of credits makes it possible to break down a qualification or the objectives of a programme of vocational education and training into units. Each unit is defined in terms of knowledge, competences and skills. It may be characterized by its size and relative importance, expressed in general by credit points (or credits) or other factors. Each unit can be validated and awarded separately.

❖ **Curriculum**

A set of actions followed when setting up a training course: it includes defining training goals, content, methods (including assessment) and material, as well as arrangements for training teachers and trainers.

❖ **Employability**

The degree of adaptability an individual demonstrates in finding and keeping a job, and updating occupational competences.

❖ **Formal learning**

Learning that occurs in an organized and structured environment (in a school/training centre or on the job) and is explicitly designated as learning (in terms of objectives, time or resources). Formal learning is intentional from the learner's point of view. It typically leads to certification.

❖ Informal learning

Learning resulting from daily activities related to work, family or leisure. It is not organized or structured in terms of objectives, time or learning support. Informal learning is in most cases unintentional from the learner's perspective. It typically does not lead to certification.

❖ Initial education/training

General or vocational education carried out in the initial education system, usually before entering working life.

❖ Comment:

some training undertaken after entry into working life may be considered as initial training (e.g. retraining) initial education and training can be carried out at any level in general or vocational education (full-time school based or alternance training) pathways or apprenticeship.

❖ Knowledge

The facts, feelings or experiences known by a person or a group of people.

❖ Labour market information system

System that provides quantitative and the qualitative information and intelligence on the labour market that can assist labour market agents in making informed plans, choices, and decisions related to their business requirements, career planning, education and training offerings, job search, recruitment, labour policies and workforce investment strategies.

❖ Learning

Learning is a cumulative process where individuals gradually assimilate increasingly complex and abstract

- entities (concepts, categories and patterns of behaviour or models) and/or acquire skills and wider.
- competences. This process takes place informally, for example through leisure activities, and in formal learning

- settings, which include the workplace.

❖ **Learning outcome**

The set of knowledge, skills and/or competences an individual has acquired and/or is able to demonstrate after completion of a learning process. Learning outcomes are statements of what a learner is expected to know, understand and/or be able to do at the end of a period of learning.

❖ **Lifelong learning**

All learning activity undertaken throughout life, with the aim of improving knowledge, skills and/or qualifications for personal, social and/or professional reasons.

❖ **Mobilizing Agency**

A Mobilizing Agency may be appointed for Recognition of Prior Learning (RPL) Projects Type 1 and 3. Trade Associations, Industry bodies, NGOs or Training Partners can be appointed as Mobilizing Agency to assist in on-ground mobilization of potential candidates to RPL camps or RPL centres.

❖ **MSDE**

The Ministry of Skill Development and Entrepreneurship of Government of India coordinates all the skill development efforts across the country.

❖ **Non-formal learning**

Learning which is embedded in planned activities not explicitly designated as learning (in terms of learning objectives, learning time or learning support), but which contain an important learning element. Non-formal learning is intentional from the learner's point of view. It normally does not lead to certification.

❖ **NOSs**

National Occupational Standards (NOSs) specify the standard of performance an individual must achieve when carrying out a particular activity at the workplace, together with the knowledge and understanding they need to meet that standard consistently. Each NOS defines one key function in a job role. In its essential form, NOS describes functions, standards of performance and knowledge/understanding.

❖ NSDC

The National Skill Development Corporation (NSDC) has been instituted to foster private sector initiatives in Skill Development. It is a Private Public Partnership (PPP) organization with representatives of Government and Industry Associations on its Board.

❖ NSQF

The National Skill Qualification Framework (NSQF) would be a descriptive framework that organizes qualifications, according to a series of levels of knowledge, skills and aptitude. These levels are defined in terms of learning outcomes, including the competencies the learners must possess regardless of whether they were acquired through formal, non-formal or informal education and training. It is, therefore, a nationally integrated education and competency based skill framework that will provide for multiple pathways both within vocational education and vocational training and among vocational education, vocational training, general education and technical education. In this way, it links one level of learning to a higher level in order to enable a person to acquire the desired skill levels, transit to the job market, and return to skill development to further upgrade their skill sets.

❖ Occupation (standard)

A set of jobs whose main tasks and duties are characterized by a high degree of similarity constitutes an occupation. Classification purposes lead to introduce the concept of 'standard occupation' to designate the 'core part of an occupation, what could be generally observed when analyzing the same occupation in different Contexts'. (ILO).

❖ Payout

It is the amount that paid out to the candidates, PIAs and SSCs, as applicable.

❖ **PMKVY**

Pradhan Mantri Kaushal Vikas Yojana (PMKVY) is the flagship scheme of MSDE. The objective of this Skill Certification scheme is to enable a large number of Indian youth to take up industry-relevant skill training that will help them in securing a better livelihood. Individuals with prior learning experience or skills will also be assessed and certified under the Recognition of Prior Learning (RPL) component of the Scheme. NSDC is the designated implementing agency for PMKVY.

❖ **Professional area**

The set of occupations, which characterize and correspond to a specific sector.

❖ **Programme (of education and training)**

An inventory of activities, learning content and/or methods implemented to achieve education or training objectives (acquiring knowledge, skills or competences), organized in a logical sequence over a specified period of time.

❖ **QPs**

A set of NOSs, aligned to a job role, called Qualification Packs (QPs), would be available for every job role in each industry sector. These drive creations of curriculum and assessments. The job roles would be at various proficiency levels and aligned to the NSQF. The NOSs and QPs for the various job roles in each sector, created by SSCs and subsequently ratified by an appropriate authority, would be available online and updated from time to time.

❖ **Qualifications**

A qualification is achieved when a competent body determines that an individual's learning has reached a specified standard of knowledge, skills and wider competences. The standard of learning outcomes is confirmed by means of an assessment process or the successful completion of a course of study. Learning and assessment for a qualification can take place through a programme of study and/or workplace experience. A qualification confers official recognition of value in the labour market and in further education and training. A qualification can be a legal entitlement to practice a trade.

❖ **Qualification authority**

Legal body in charge of establishing, maintaining and promoting the qualification framework.

❖ **Qualifications framework**

A qualifications framework is an instrument for the development and classification of qualifications according to a set of criteria for levels of learning achieved. This set of criteria may be implicit in the qualifications' descriptors themselves or made explicit in the form of a set of level descriptors. The scope of frameworks may be comprehensive of all learning achievement and pathways or may be confined to a particular sector, for example initial education, adult education and training or an occupational area. Some frameworks may have more design elements and a tighter structure than others; some may have a legal basis whereas others represent a consensus of views of social partners. All qualifications frameworks, however, establish a basis for improving the quality, accessibility, linkages and public or labour market recognition of qualifications within a country and internationally.

❖ **Qualification system**

Qualifications systems include all aspects of a country's activity that result in the recognition of learning. These systems include the means of developing and operationalizing national or regional policy on qualifications, institutional arrangements, quality assurance processes, assessment and awarding processes, skills recognition and other mechanisms that link education and training to the labour market and civil society. Qualifications systems may be more or less integrated and coherent. One feature of a qualifications system may be an explicit framework of qualifications.

❖ **Quality**

Quality refers to the inherent or distinctive characteristics or properties of a person, object, process or other thing. Such characteristics or properties may set a person or thing apart from other persons or things, or may denote some degree of achievement or excellence.

❖ **Recognition (of competences)**

1. Formal recognition: The process of granting official status to skills and competences either

- through the award of certificates or
- through the grant of equivalence, credit units, validation of gained skills and/or competences and/or.

2. Social recognition: The acknowledgement of the value of skills and/or competences by economic and social stakeholders.

❖ **Regulated profession**

Professional activity or group of professional activities access to which, and the practice of which (or to one of its forms) is directly or indirectly subject to legislative, regulatory or administrative provisions concerning the possession of specific professional qualifications.

❖ **RPL**

Recognition of Prior Learning (RPL) is the process of recognizing previous learning, often experiential, towards gaining a qualification.

❖ **RPL Facilitator**

RPL Facilitators are SSC approved trainers who have completed the Training of Trainers (ToT) programme. For conduct of a RPL Project, SSC shall appoint such trainers to undertake Counselling and Pre-Screening, Orientation and Bridge Courses, where applicable. There should be no overlap in the functions of the Assessment Agency and the RPL Facilitator engaged for a project.

❖ **SDMS**

The Skill Development Management System (SDMS) is the IT solution that has been developed and maintained by the NSDC.

❖ **Sector**

The term sector is used either to define a category of companies on the basis of their main economic activity, product or technology (chemistry, tourism) or as a transversal/horizontal occupational category (ICT, marketing or Human resources).

❖ **Comment**

The following distinctions are common:

1. Between public sector (government at various levels and government-controlled bodies) and private sector (private business).
2. between primary sector (agriculture, forestry, fishing, hunting, mining and quarrying*), secondary sector (manufacturing industry, gas and electricity, water supply, construction*) and tertiary sector (services, e.g. transport, storage, communication, trade, financing and insurance, as well as the public sector*).

❖ **Sectoral qualification**

A qualification implemented by a group of companies belonging to the same sector in order to meet common training needs.

❖ **Skill**

The knowledge and experience needed to perform a specific task or job.

❖ **Social dialogue**

A process of exchange between social partners to promote consultation, dialogue and collective bargaining.

❖ **Comment:**

1. social dialogue can be bipartite (involving representatives of workers and employers) or tripartite (also associating public authorities and/or representatives of civil society, NGOs, etc.);
2. social dialogue can take place at various levels (company, sectoral /cross-sectoral and local/regional/national/ transnational);
3. at international level, social dialogue can be bilateral, trilateral or multilateral, according to the number of countries involved.

❖ **Special Areas**

The special areas designated by the Government of India include the Left Wing Extremism worst affected districts, Jammu & Kashmir, North-East Region (8 States), Lakshadweep, Himachal Pradesh, Uttarakhand, and Andaman & Nicobar Islands.

❖ **Special Groups**

In context of PMKVY, special group includes women candidates and persons with disability (PwD).

❖ **SSCs**

Sector Skill Councils (SSCs) are industry-led bodies, who would be responsible for defining the skilling needs, concept, processes, certification and accreditation of their respective industry sectors. The SSCs shall prescribe the NOSs and QPs for the various job roles relevant to their industry, classify the job roles and shall work with the National Skill Development Agency (NSDA) to ensure that these are in accordance with the National Skill Qualification Framework (NSQF).

❖ **Stakeholder**

A person or organization that has a legitimate interest in a project or entity. In discussing the decision-making process for institutions-including large business corporations, government agencies and non-profit organizations--the concept has been broadened to include everyone with an interest (or "stake") in what the entity does.

❖ **Validation of informal / non-formal learning**

The process of assessing and recognizing a wide range of knowledge, know-how, skills and competences which people develop throughout their lives in different contexts, for example through education, work and leisure activities.

❑❑❑

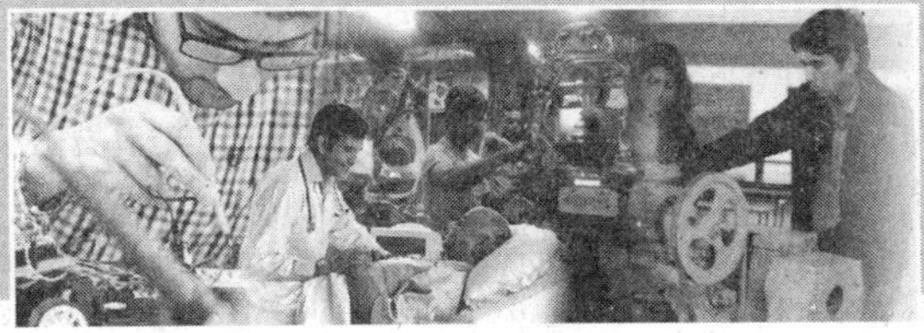

FAQs

Why should India focus on Skill Development?

India is one of the few countries in the world where the working age population will be far in excess of those dependent on them and, as per the World Bank, this will continue for at least three decades till 2040. This has increasingly been recognized as a potential source of significant strength for the national economy, provided we are able to equip and continuously upgrade the skills of the population in the working age group. In recognition of this need, the Government of India has adopted skill development as a national priority over the next 10 years.

How is the skill development initiative organized in India?

NSDA is the key coordinating body for skills development in India. NSDC is an organization setup in the PPP mode to execute skill development initiatives. It has three key roles—create, fund and develop an ecosystem by promoting the role of the private sector and the employers in skill development. Other Central government ministries and State governments have a focus on skill development within the purview of their domain. NGOs and the Private Sector also contribute to the overall initiative. Sector Skill Councils have been set up to standardize the occupational standards, they are responsible for certification, train the trainers and accreditation. They also participate in the creation of the Labour market information system by developing LMIS for their sectors. A Cabinet Committee on Skill Development with representation from various ministries and NSDA drives the policy formulation on skill development.

How is the management of skill development organized within India? What is NSDA?

The Government of India has setup the National Skill Development Agency (NSDA) as an autonomous body which will coordinate and harmonize the skill development efforts of the Government and the private sector to achieve the skilling targets of the 12th Plan and beyond. The Central Ministries and National Skill Development Corporation will continue to implement schemes in their remit. The NSDA will anchor the National Skills Qualifications Framework (NSQF) and facilitate the setting up of professional certifying bodies in addition to the existing ones. NSDA has subsumed the three earlier bodies of Office of Advisor to PM on Skill Development, National Council of Skill Development and National Skill Development Coordination Board.

With NSDA's role being one of harmonization and coordination, how will its recommendations be mandated and complied to?

NSDA is the main coordinating body for skill development in the country and has been tasked with the responsibility of streamlining, rationalizing and integrating the skill development efforts across various ministries and departments in the centre and state. Any proposal related to skill development would require the NSDA viewpoint to be considered before the same can be put up before the Cabinet or any committee of the Cabinet for approval. The Chairman NSDA is also a permanent invitee to meetings of the Cabinet Committee on Skill Development.

What is the National Skill Development Corporation? What role does NSDC play in skill development?

The National Skill Development Corporation (NSDC) is a Public Private Partnership, The NSDC was formed by leading industry associations and the Government as a Public Private Partnership to catalyse and enhance the role of the corporate and private sector in skill Development. The NSDC funds skill development initiatives, Sector Skill Councils and other activities related to skill development including the setting-up of large scale, for-profit sustainable vocational institutions in the country, by encouraging private sector participation and providing low-cost funding for training capacity. NSDC is also responsible for India's participation in the World Skills Competition.

How are other Central Government departments involved in skill development?

In the Central Government, different Ministries are closely involved in skill development. These ministries mainly operate in following ways—through setting up own training capacity in specific sectors (examples of such ministries include MoLE, Ministry of Agriculture, Ministry of Health and Family Welfare, etc.) or through providing per-trainee costs of training for specific target populations (examples of such ministries include Ministry of Rural Development, Ministry of Women and Child Development, etc.).

How are the State Governments involved in skill development?

Most State Governments have set up State Skill Development Missions (SSDM) as nodal bodies to anchor the skill development agenda in the State. SSDMs are expected to play a significant role in escalating the pace of skilling, through identification of key sectors for skill development in the State, as well as coordinating with Central Ministries and Stateline Departments, as well as industry and private training organizations. The erstwhile PM National Council for Skill Development (PMNCSD) now subsumed within NSDA has helped states like Uttar Pradesh to create a State Skill Development Policy. It has helped other states such as Assam, Arunachal Pradesh, Nagaland, Manipur, Odisha and Himachal Pradesh on their skill development efforts.

What is India's target for skill development?

The national target for skill development is 500 Million (50 crores) by 2022. The target for the 12th Five Year Plan is 5 crores. For the financial year i.e. FY 2013-2014, a target of 72.8 lakhs persons has been set. This target has been accepted by various central government ministries and NSDC.

How much money are various central government organizations spending towards skill development?

Ministries such as Rural Development, Housing and Urban Poverty Alleviation (HUPA), Textiles, Medium, Small and Micro Enterprises (MSME), Labour & Employment (MoLE) and Tourism have separate budgets for skill development schemes run by them. In respect of central sector schemes and centrally sponsored schemes that are meant for the welfare of certain socio-economic groups, there is an effort to ensure that at least 10 per cent of the funds under these schemes are earmarked for skill development activities. The Government has also set up the National Skill Development Fund (NSDF). While the government had contributed to the NSDF, the NSDF would also be a receptacle of multilateral, bilateral and private sector funds for skill development. The fund is managed through a Trust.

What is the National Skill Qualification Framework?

The National Skill Qualification Framework (NSQF) is a national integrated competency based framework covering the education sector, the vocational and technical education sector that would provide for accumulation and transfer of credits including recognition of prior learning both within and across education including technical education and vocational training. It would provide for progression from one level to another both horizontal and vertical so that persons can build up on their qualifications throughout their lifetime.

When will the National Skill Qualification Framework be released?

NSQF builds on two draft frameworks, namely National Vocational Education Qualification Framework (NVEQF) prepared by MHRD and National Vocational Qualification Framework (NVQF) prepared by MoLE. NSDA has further detailed this document based on various reviews and submitted the draft NSQF for inter-ministerial consultation. It is expected that the NSQF will be approved in the next 3-4 months.

How has skill development been integrated into National Service Scheme?

The National Service Scheme has been in existence for quite some time and is a vehicle for engaging students in real, long term projects partnering with other stakeholders in society such as NGOs, Corporates, Foundations and Educational Institutions. A pilot involving a three year program to include vocational skill education as part of NSS is being conducted in 10 universities across the country. This pilot will initially touch 30,000 students and once launched nationally will impact 32 lakhs students every year.

Do Banks provide financial credit for vocational education?

Non-availability of credit from formal channels was one of the long felt constraints in scaling up vocational courses. To address this issue, the erstwhile National Council on Skill Development set up a committee to come up with a draft policy on making skill training eligible for credit support. As a result of this, the Indian Banks' Association (IBA) has approved a 'Model Loan Scheme for Vocational Education and Training' and circulated to its member banks for adoption and implementation. As part of this scheme, banks can finance an amount varying from INR 20,000 to INR 1 50,000 depending on the duration of the course. The detailed circular from IBA on this scheme is available here.

What is the Credit Guarantee Fund?

The Ministry of Finance has announced the setting up of a vocational loan credit guarantee fund. The credit guarantee fund for skill development will facilitate the process of bankers willing to lend to individuals seeking funding for undertaking skill development programmes. The credit guarantee fund will ensure that in the event of such a loan going bad, despite the normal precautions having been taken by the bank, the latter will not suffer, and can seek restitution from the fund. NSDA is working with the Ministry of Finance to support the 'Model Loan Scheme for Vocational Training' launched by IBA.

Are vocational courses exempt from Service Tax?

The erstwhile Office of the Advisor to Prime Minister on Skill Development has worked with the Ministry of Finance to include important categories of vocational courses training a significant number of people in the exemption list of Service Tax. Consequently a circular has been issued by the Ministry of Finance and these courses have been exempted from Service Tax. A copy of the aforesaid circular is available here. The Ministry of Finance has also exempted services provided by NSDC, SSCs and schemes approved by NSDC from service tax.

How is the Apprenticeship Act being modified?

The earlier Apprenticeship Training Scheme had low adoptions due to certain rigidities and low trainee stipends. The Ministry of Labour and Employment is exploring radical changes to make the Apprenticeship act more industry and employee friendly.

What is NSDA doing for the Construction Sector which is one of the largest employment sectors in the country?

Under the Building and Other Construction Workers' Welfare Cess Act (BOCW), a total of INR 7,057 crores have been collected by State Level Welfare Boards. Of this only 14 per cent of the funds have been utilized. Based on erstwhile PMNCSD's inputs, inputs, MoLE has mandated that 20 per cent of the BOCW funds should be used for activities related to skill development of the registered construction workers and their dependents.

What is the Rashtriya Kaushal Puraskar?

NSDA proposes to launch the National Skill Awards (Rashtriya Kaushal Puraskar) to recognize outstanding achievements of individuals as well as institutional entities such as central ministries, State Skill Development Missions, Training Institutions, Public and Private Enterprises in the skill development space. This will help to create a positive and aspirational image around skill development.

What is the Rural Broadband Initiative? How can this be used in Skill Development?

The Rural Broadband initiative of the Ministry of IT and Communications proposes to connect 250,000 *panchayats* in India using high capacity broadband connectivity of atleast 100 Mbps. Riding on this technology highway, skill centres can be established at *panchayats* and skilling content can be delivered digitally. Pilots for this are being planned in Vizag, North Tripura and Ajmer before a larger rollout.

What are Citizen Service Centre's and how can they contribute to Skill Development?

CSCs are the Citizen Service Centre's set up under the Ministry of IT & Communications to provide prescribed citizen services including in the villages. These centres are being used both to deliver skill development through IT and also as centres for skill development.

What are the steps taken to ensure inclusiveness of the skill development initiatives?

NSDA is working with various ministries to coordinate inclusiveness of the skill development initiative in the country. This covers:

- Geographical inclusiveness in terms of target states such as Jammu & Kashmir, North Eastern States, Tribal Areas, Rural Belts and Urban Belts and LWE areas
- Economic inclusiveness in terms of schemes for unemployed, underemployed, people below poverty line, rural poor and urban poor
- Gender inclusive in terms of schemes specifically focused on women
- Demographic inclusiveness in terms of schemes focused on youths, school dropouts, uneducated, adult literacy, etc.
- Caste based inclusiveness in terms of schemes focused on SC/ST and other minorities

What role will Employment Exchanges play in Skill Develop-ment?

Currently, employment exchanges have become just repositories of lists of unemployed persons. NSDA is working with the States to improve the functioning of the exchanges and also explore alternate roles for them. Various states are considering to convert the current Employment Exchanges into District Career Guidance and Counselling Centres, in which capacity, the exchanges can play a crucial role in skill development. These exchanges are leveraging technology to increase their reach to the stakeholders. They are changing to provide guidance to individuals and mentoring aspiring individuals on entrepreneurship and self-employment. They are working in a PPP mode to effectively leverage the technology and process knowhow of private sector organizations. An example is the Karnataka State Employment Exchange initiative.

How is the private sector involved in skill development initiatives?

Private Sector plays a key role in skill development. A majority of the skill development programmes of various Central Ministries and State Missions are delivered by the private sector. For example Private organizations are adopting ITIs, leading and participating in their management boards and benchmarking the training courses and curriculums in these ITIs to be suitable for industry requirements. An initiative of this scale cannot be successful without a significantly increased participation from the private sector especially since a large percentage of skill demand is in this sector. The government realizes this and is engaging in a PPP mode where relevant to make this a success. NSDC is a body setup in the PPP mode to catalyse and increase the active participation of the private sector in skill development including the building of training capacity. Sector Skill Councils are setup with participation from industry bodies and private employers to standardize trade and competency definitions and as a part of the larger strategy to get employers to lead skill development efforts. Private training organizations, NGOs are being funded by NSDC to increase their training capacity.

How is the government incentivizing the private sector to participate in skill development?

There are a variety of incentives for private sector to participate in skill development these include:

Weighted deduction from income tax for specified investments in skill development in the agriculture, manufacturing and services sector. This was originally applicable for the manufacturing sector organizations. At the behest of the erstwhile O/o APM, this was extended to include the service sector organizations

- Exemption from Service Tax.
- Expenditure on employment linked vocational training to qualify as CSR expenditure.
- Grants to the private sector to conduct skill development programmes under different Central Government and State Government Schemes and by NSDC.
- Low cost funding to set up sustainable skill development initiatives through NSDC.

What role can MPs/MLAs play in skill development?

India is organized into 543 parliamentary constituencies and 4,120 assembly constituencies. MPs and MLAs from these constituencies have the advantage of being most closely involved with these constituencies. They can play an active role in bringing together relevant stakeholders (training providers, employers, NGOs, local people) and resources (local infrastructure, funds) and catalyse skill development in these constituencies. This has been done successfully in few constituencies and can be scaled to many more. Local Area development funds could be used to upgrade or provide infrastructure for skill development.

What are the various sources of funds for skill development?

Funds for skill development are available from multiple sources. Funds available for individuals through Loans for vocational education from banks, Reward such as the STAR scheme, Grants, Scholarships from Ministry of Minority Affairs, National SC / ST Finance Corporations, etc., Voucher programmes run by State Governments (e.g. Gujarat) and Construction workers Cess. Funds are available for Skill Development Providers from Central & State Governments and NSDC. Other organizations that provide funding for both individuals and skill development organizations include Trusts, NGOs, International foundations, CSR funds from corporate, Corporate Sector, High net worth individuals and Development agencies.

What is the community college initiative? How does it aid skill development?

Community colleges are aimed at supplementing mainstream education by providing alternate pathways to professional growth. Offerings could include vocational courses that enhance employability of students. MHRD announced the launch of 200 pilot colleges in 2012 after a series of events in 2011 built momentum for implementation of a more broad-based role for community colleges in the Indian system of higher education. This was unanimously endorsed in the State Education Ministers' Conference held on 22nd February 2012, and a Committee of 9 Education Ministers of States was constituted to finalize the concept and framework of the Community College scheme. Main objectives of the scheme are:

- To provide career oriented skills education to students currently pursuing higher education but are actually interested in entering the workforce at the earliest opportunity;
- To provide opportunities for employable and certifiable skills with necessary general education to high school pass-outs not ready to enrol in traditional colleges while also providing them a path to transfer to higher education including technical education programmes;

- To provide opportunities for up-gradation and certification of traditional / acquired skills of the learners irrespective of her / his qualification or age; and
- To provide opportunities for community–based life-long learning by offering courses of general interest to the community for personal development and interest.

What is the focus for sensitive areas such as North East, J&K, etc.?

NSDA is working with the relevant central ministries and state governments to drive specific initiatives for such areas for example, in the North East, industry partnerships with ITIs are being setup in trades such as driving, health and beauty, hospitality. Assam was among the first states to pilot NVEQF in government schools. In J&K, the Udaan scheme of the Ministry of Finance has enabled industry partnerships that aims to train and place students in mainstream jobs. Different Ministries have focused programmes for the sensitive areas:

- In J&K: MHRD, MoRD Himayat, Ministry of Labour & Employment–ITI's, Ministry of Home Affairs & NSDC Udaan, The J&K State Skill Mission
- In North East: Ministry of Labour, Ministry of housing and Poverty Alleviation, North East Council, Department of North East Region, State Skills Missions, NSDC
- In select districts: MoRD Roshni, NSDC, State Skill Missions

How will the proposed World Class Skill Centre in Delhi change the vocational education landscape?

The World Class Skill Centre is a collaborative effort between the Delhi Government and Singapore Government to setup a 10,000 annual capacity training institution benchmarked to international standards. This centre will have 50 faculty members trained in Singapore and a residential campus for 3000 students. This centre will leverage the help of Ministry of Education, Singapore in curriculum design, teacher training, training pedagogy and some aspects of infrastructure creation. This centre will contribute to establishing a new modern image for vocational education in the country.

What is the relevance of a Labour Market Information System (LMIS)? When will a National level LMIS be available for India?

LMIS is critical to provide accurate data around skill demand, skill supply, the gap therein and skilling capacity across the country. Information derived from LMIS will be useful to drive policy formulation and planning the skill development initiatives. The NSDA is coordinating the development of a National level LMIS which would probably become fully operational in a five year timeframe. In that time, all states, central ministries, as well as public stakeholders ranging from individuals seeking training or employment opportunities, potential employers looking for skilled personnel, training providers offering their services, etc. would be using the LMIS to link up with others in the chain. In the interim, the SSCs are developing LMIS for their sectors and these would integrate with the LMIS when rolled out.

How can large PSU's efforts in skill development be aligned? How will NSDA support these efforts?

NSDA is engaged with PSUs to facilitate skill development in a variety of ways:

- Making available their spare/underutilized space and equipment for skill development
- Donating their obsolete equipment to training institutions to facilitate hands-on training
- Taking on a large number of trade apprentices so that these young men and women get real on-the-job training
- PSUs of each sector coming together to create at least one iconic national training centre for the training in skills needed for their sector. In a meeting of the PSUs, held on 3rd Sept, the oil and gas sector PSUs agreed to set up one such centre for training in the skills needed for the exploration, production, refining and marketing of petroleum products
- Encouraging that of all manpower engaged under their contracts, a certain minimum percentage are skilled and certified
- Encouraging that 10 per cent to 15 per cent of their CSR funds are used exclusively for funding skill development training of individuals from each PSUs target area.

What is your vision on Governance of the whole skilling effort given that millions of tax payers' rupees are being pumped in? How will accountability and transparency be brought in?

NSDA is conscious that this is a major area of concern. NSDA has proposed amendments to the National Policy of Skill Development, which would require outcomes based approach:

- At least 70 per cent of persons trained through any scheme would need to be either self-employment or placed in employment by the training provider.
- NSDA is seeking to establish a relationship between the cost of training and the incremental earning capacity of the trained individual. While a sector-wise study for the same is proposed with the ADB, anecdotal evidence seems to suggest that for many entry level jobs, the cost of training should not exceed the aggregate amount of incremental earning that the trainee would get in three months.
- Benchmarking skill development efforts across states and Ministries.
- Publishing results of skill development on the website.

How does NSDC function?

NSDC is a not-for-profit company set up by the Ministry of Finance, under Section 25 of the Companies Act. It has an equity base of INR 10 crore, of which the private sector holds 51 per cent, while the Government of India controls 49 per cent. This makes NSDC a one-of-its-kind public private partnership in skill development education in India.

The corporation has a tiered structure—a 15-member Board and the National Skill Development Fund (NSDF), a 100 per cent government-owned trust—which work in sync to fulfil the NSDC's strategic objectives.

What is the target for skill development set for NSDC?

NSDC has been set a target to create capacity and train 15 crores persons by the year 2022. For the current financial year FY14, NSDC has a target to train 10 lakhs persons.

What is the key role played by NSDC?

NSDC's key roles are:

- Funding and incentivizing skill development programmes and Sector Skill councils
- Enabling support services such as innovation, skill gap and other studies, train the trainer programmes and international collaboration
- Shaping/creating a sustainable ecosystem for skill development

How does an organization obtain funding from NSDC?

NSDC calls for proposals in select areas (sectors/utilities) from time to time. To receive funding, an organization needs to submit a proposal in response to the call for a proposal. Proposals are invited from private players, industry bodies, entrepreneurs and NGOs in a prescribed template. Currently NSDC has an ongoing call for proposals for both training initiatives and innovation programmes. Once the organization receives a proposal, it will be evaluated thoroughly. It will be accepted for funding based on the organization's evaluation and subject to clearance by the NSDC Board. After the funding is granted, the NSDC will continuously monitor the use of funds, the progress of the project and impact on skill development.

What are the criteria for consideration of proposals by NSDC?

NSDC seeks proposals that target scarce skill sets or student populations with huge unmet needs and focuses on large-scale, high-quality training institutes both that require funding and those that do not. Some criteria used for evaluation of proposals are:

- Sustainability of business model in the long term.
- Usage of technology and innovation to have a 'multiplier' effect on skill development.
- Proposals leveraging existing infrastructure are preferred.
- Partnerships with prospective employers, state governments and financial institutions.
- Predetermined outcomes and milestones.

Does NSDC provide training for candidates?

NSDC currently does not carry out any training or skill development activities directly. NSDC is primarily focusing on enabling the skill development ecosystem by bringing in key stakeholders together such as government, NGOs, employers both private sector and the public sector, etc. NSDC is funding independently employer led sector skill councils create National Occupation Standards, to standardize trades and courses and certify candidates coming out of the NSDC partner organizations. NSDC is catalysing skill development by providing funding to organizations interested in setting up training centres.

Which sectors does the NSDC provide services for?

Currently, the NSDC provides services for the following sectors in India:

- Automobile/Auto components
- Electronics hardware
- Textiles and garments
- Leather and leather goods
- Chemicals and pharmaceuticals
- Gems and jewellery
- Building and construction
- Food processing
- Handlooms and handicrafts
- Building hardware and home furnishings
- IT or software
- ITES-BPO
- Tourism, hospitality and travel
- Transportation/ logistics/ warehousing and packaging
- Organized retail
- Real estate
- Media,entertainment,broadcasting,contentcreation,animation
- Healthcare
- Banking/ insurance and finance
- Education/ skill development
- Unorganized sector
- Infrastructure

What is a Sector Skill Council?

Sector Skill Councils (SSCs) are national partnership organizations that bring together all the stakeholders–industry, labour and the academia for the purpose of workforce development for particular industry sectors. The National Skill Policy 2009 outlines the role of SSCs. The SSCs will play a significant role in setting up and determining skills, competency standards and qualifications for various jobs, which can be used by companies to assess employee performance and skill development needs. These can also be used to prepare training programmes and job profiles. The SSCs will forecast changes in the labour market and will enable the standardization of affiliation and accreditation processes. The SSCs also carry out affiliation of training partners that wish to partner NSDC but do not have the scale to be a direct partner of NSDC. The SSCs will work with assessors and assessment agencies' would also certify the candidates and maintain a national skills register for their sector.

How many Sector Skill Councils have been set up?

NSDC has been entrusted with the responsibility of setting up SSCs across various sectors. As of date, 26 SSCs have been approved by NSDC and this includes sectors such as Automotive, Security, Retail, Media & Entertainment, IT-ITeS, Healthcare, BFSI, etc.

What is a National Occupational Standard?

National Occupational Standards (NOS) specify the standard of performance an individual must achieve when carrying out a function in the workplace, together with the knowledge and understanding they need to meet that standard consistently. For example is a welder's required competency profile and job profile defined in a standardized manner across the country? Each NOS defines one key function in a job role. The NOS are laid down by employers (through their SSCs). A set of NOS, aligned to a job role, called Qualification Pack (QP), would be available for every job role in each industry sector. These drive both the creation of curriculum, and assessments.

How do I understand the skill requirement in a particular sector or geography?

NSDC engages organizations to conduct studies to understand the geographical and sector wise skill requirements across the country.

How many Training Partners have been approved by NSDC?

As of 4th October 2013, a total of 101 training partners have been approved by NSDC of which 58 Training Partners are currently active subsequent to being assessed and approved by NSDC.

What is the training capacity created by NSDC as on date?

In the last 3 years, NSDC has approved 101 training institutions to create a current annual training capacity of 16M. This is a large jump over the current annual training capacity in India, which is a little over 5M. As of 27th September 2013, NSDC has committed funds of INR 1986 crores over the next three years towards the approved training institutions.

What is NSDC's role in the WorldSkills Initiative?

WorldSkills India, an initiative of NSDC, organizes a skills competition in India to decide the Indian representation for chosen disciplines at the WorldSkills International competition held in different countries. WorldSkills India is the official body representing the country at WorldSkills International competition. India competes in chosen skills categories at the WorldSkills competition. India has so far participated twice in WorldSkills competitions held in London in 2011 and Leipzig in 2013.

What are the advocacy initiatives done by NSDC for skill development?

NSDC carries out advocacy initiatives at different levels including:

- National Associations like ASSOCHAM, CII, FICCI, EFI, FISME, etc.
- National Sectoral Associations including the 7 stakeholder organizations
- State Level Chambers and SME organizations
- International bilateral and multilateral agencies
- Trusts, Foundations, NGO's
- Youth organizations, colleges and other educational institutions
- Corporates both public and private sector including MNCs
- MP's & MLAs
- State Skill missions
- Central ministries

NSDC is also in the process of launching a national campaign and had engaged the Market Research Agency Firefly Millward Brown to conduct a study on aspirations and barriers connected with skills. This study aims to understand the perception of the common man regarding vocational skills. Inputs from this study are being channelled into a nationwide marketing campaign being designed by Ogilvy & Mathers (O&M). In addition to this, initiatives such as WorldSkills above and the National Skills Awards will also help in improving the image of vocational skills. The National Skill Qualification Framework will create an equivalence mechanism between vocational education and academic education. This will further help position skill development in the mainstream.

What is the STAR Scheme?

The Finance Minister in his Budget Speech of 2013 proposed a scheme to encourage skill development for youth by providing monetary rewards for successful completion of approved training programs. This scheme titled 'The National Skill Certification and Monetary Reward Scheme', also known as the STAR Scheme, rewards candidates undergoing skill training by authorized institutions at an average monetary reward of INR 10,000 per candidate. The scheme targets to benefit 10 lakhs youth at an approximate cost of INR 1,000 crores.

What are the skill development initiatives available in Jammu & Kashmir?

In 2011, two flagship schemes—Himayat and Udaan—were launched to promote skill development in J&K. Himayat, under the Ministry of Rural Development (MoRD), aims to train and place 1, 00,000 J&K youth over five years through private training providers in entry-level jobs. Udaan, on the other hand, aims to train and place 40,000 J&K youth over five years. The scheme is funded by the Ministry of Home Affairs (MHA) and is targeted at graduates and post-graduates, who are trained and placed by corporate partners outside J&K.

What is the learning from Udaan so far? How can the accountability of corporates in Udaan be strengthened?

Udaan is seeing the nation's top corporates such as Godrej, Tata, HCL, etc. partner actively to provide the youth of J&K the best-in-class training and exposure to their facilities. This would be the first step in orienting the youth to a corporate environment. However there are several socio-cultural issues that need sensitization such as expectation management of the youth, managing cultural divergences, addressing parental concerns, etc.

What facilities are available to the Scheduled Caste for skill development?

Persons from the Scheduled Castes constitute about 16.2 per cent of the total population in India (Census 2011) and are some of the most marginalized sections of the society. There is a critical need to ensure that youth from these communities get access to education and skill-building opportunities. The Government of India in the Ministry of Social Justice and Empowerment is implementing a 'Central Sector Scheme of Special Central Assistance (SCA) to Scheduled Castes Sub Plan (SCSP) since 1980 for the development of Scheduled Castes. In a revised guideline released in May 2013, the Government has mandated that the State Governments/UTs should use at least 10 per cent of these funds for skill development Programmes in order to enhance the employability of the target group. National SC/ST Finance Corporations has the mandate of providing concessional finance for setting up of self-employment projects and skill-training grants to unemployed SC persons living below Double the Poverty Line.

What facilities are available to the tribals for skill development?

The Ministry of Tribal Affairs has launched a scheme for 'Vocational Training Centres in Tribal Areas' to encourage the setting of training centres in tribal areas and offering vocational courses appropriate to the employment potential of the area. Under this scheme, a maximum assistance of INR 30,000 per annum per ST trainee is provided.

What is the National Urban Livelihoods Mission?

National Urban Livelihoods Mission (NULM) or Sharna Jayanti Shagari Rozgar Yojana (SJSRY) scheme is aimed at providing gainful employment to the unemployed or under-employed urban poor by encouraging skill development and self-employment. This scheme benefits about 2 lakhs urban poor under skill development and 50,000 under self-employment annually.

What is the National Rural Livelihoods Mission?

National Rural Livelihoods Mission (NRLM) or Ajeevika (earlier known as Swarnajayanti Grameen Swarozgar Yojana) scheme is aimed at reducing poverty by enabling poor households to access gainful self-employment and skilled wage employment opportunities. Ajeevika focuses on organizing rural BPL households into Self Help Groups and providing them training to set up their own micro enterprise. 20 per cent of NRLM funds are available for placement linkedskill development.

What is the Modular Employable Skills scheme?

Modular Employable Skills (MES) scheme, under the aegis of the Ministry of Labour and Employment, aims to provide vocational training using demand driven short term training courses created in consultation with the industry. MES courses can have duration of as low as 90 hours. Training fees of candidates who successfully complete the training are refunded by the government. This scheme is also known as the Skill Development Initiative Scheme (SDIS).

What is the Jan Shikshan Sansthan scheme?

Jan Shikshan Sansthan (JSS), under the National Literacy Mission, is a unique scheme crafted by the Government of India focusing on the poor, the illiterates, the neo-literates, the under-privileged and the un-reached. The Jan Shikshan Sansthans are unique in that they do not provide just skill development, but link literacy with vocational skills and provide large doses of Life Enrichment Education (LEE) to the people. The Jan Shikshan Sansthans offer a large number (371) of vocational training programmes from candle making to computer courses.

What is the Vocationalization of Secondary Education scheme?

The Centrally Sponsored Scheme (CSS) 'Vocationalization of Secondary Education' was launched by the MHRD to strengthen vocational education in Classes XI–XII. Pilots in Class IX and XI have been started to incorporate vocational education in schools.

What is the Saakshar Bharat scheme?

Saakshar Bharat, a centrally sponsored scheme of Department of School Education and Literacy (DSEL), Ministry of Human Resource Development (MHRD), Government of India (GOI), was launched on the International Literacy Day, 8th September, 2009. It aims to further promote and strengthen Adult Education, specially of women, by extending educational options to those adults who having lost the opportunity of access to formal education and crossed the standard age for receiving such education, now feel a need for learning of any type, including, literacy, basic education (equivalency to formal education), vocational education (skill development), physical and emotional development, practical arts, applied science, sports, and recreation.

What are the skill development facilities available for the North Eastern States?

Various Ministries have skill initiatives in North East. These include—Ministry of Labour, Ministry of Housing and Poverty Alleviation, North East Council, Department of North East Region, State Skills Missions and NSDC. The Ministry of Labour and Employment (MoLE) has sanctioned a new centrally sponsored scheme 'Enhancing Skill Development Infrastructure in North East States and Sikkim' to upgrade 20 ITIs and supplement deficient infrastructure in 28 ITIs at an overall budget of INR 57.4 crores. The Ministry of Development of North Eastern Region is focusing on the socio-economic development of the North Eastern region and driving various developmental initiatives for this region.

What are some examples of skill development initiatives in the North Eastern States?

Such examples include:

- ITIs in Assam, Meghalaya, Nagaland, Arunachal Pradesh, Mizoram, Sikkim and Tripura revamped and upgraded in partnership with private sector organizations like Tata Motors, VLCC, HUL
- NVEQF pilot launched in schools in partnership with Pearson India and IndiaCan
- UK-India Education Research Initiative (UKIERI) driven project to upgrade hospitality training in 5 ITIs in Assam in partnership with Westminster Kingsway College
- The private sector has also initiated a number of programmes in the North East through NSDC.

How are the minority segments addressed in the skill development initiative?

The Ministry of Minority Affairs has launched multiple schemes to address the skill development and enhance the employability of the minority segment. The Multi-Sectoral Development Programme (MSDP) has a component for skill development and the ministry has earmarked at least 10 per cent of the funds for skill development. The 'Learn and Earn' scheme, also known as 'Seekho Aur Kamao', is a 100 per cent Central Sector Scheme having the two components of placement linked skills training for modern trades and skills training program for traditional trades/arts/craft forms. The scheme 'Nai Roshni' for 'Leadership Development of Minority Women' specifically focuses on providing knowledge, tools and techniques to enable minority women to become self-reliant and independent.

What is the focus on skill development of women?

The Ministry of Women and Child Development has numerous schemes focusing on the development and empowerment of women and children. Some of these include the Kishori Shakti Yojana, Rajiv Gandhi Scheme for Empowerment of Adolescent Girls (RGSEAG)–SABLA, Swayam Siddha and Support to Training and Empowerment Programme for Women (STEP).

What is the focus on skill development for people with disabilities (PWD)?

Skill Development for PWD at the Central Government level is primarily led by Ministry of Social Justice & Empowerment and various bodies under MSJE which work for welfare of people with different disabilities such as National Trust. At the State level there are programs and schemes run for providing vocational training courses for PWD within the State. Since the numbers of PWD in India are large—estimates range between 40–70 million, the NSDC thought process is to promote models which are outcome driven, aligned to existing job roles and which move to sustainability over time. Towards this NSDC has supported Arunim, an NGO under National Trust (MSJE), to design run and monitor a business plan competition for NGOs who train and employ PWD to develop capability to develop viable business models for NGOs built around products made by PWD.

What is the average cost per candidate for skill development?

The average cost per candidate for skill development varies on the basis of the nature of the skilling course as well as the duration of the course.

What is the wage that a candidate can expect to earn after undergoing skill training?

The wage for a candidate depends on the specific trade in which he/she has been skilled as well as the location of the workplace. The laws of demand and supply also play a role in determining the wages offered for any job. The NSDA is urging the State Governments to create sufficient differential in the minimum wages between unskilled and semi-skilled; and between semi-skilled and skilled, so that the necessary incentives for getting skilled exists. The NSDA is also proposing a sector-wise study to link the cost of training to the likely wages that should be earned after the training is done. Anecdotal evidence suggests that for most entry level jobs in the services sector, the cost of the training should not exceed the aggregate amount that would be earned by the trained individual in the first three months of employment.

Does a candidate have to move out of his home location for skill training or a job?

A vast network of training organizations including ITIs, VTPs and private training providers are available in almost every district of the country to provide skill training. A candidate can approach any nearby organization and enrol for skill training. Based on the demand for the skill in his home location, the candidate can get a job in proximity to his home or may be required to travel outside. A candidate can increase his earning potential by skilling himself in a high demand sector and taking up a job in a high demand geography.

Does vocational education also include some soft skills based education?

Soft skills such as basic literacy, personal grooming, financial management, people interaction, healthy living, etc. are a necessity to achieve growth in life. Vocational standards and education curriculum being devised by SSCs and training partners are incorporating soft skill based courses as part of the curriculum.

What is the earliest age for vocational education?

Under the Right to Education Act, a child until the age of 14 years must be in school. After the age of 14, a child can be employed as an apprentice in non-hazardous occupations. However, the minimum age at which most organizations are willing to engage workers is 18 years.

Are there options for self-employment for a candidate after skill training?

One of the intentions of skill training is to make the person more confident in his abilities and equip him with the necessary skills for self-employment. There are specific skills training courses that nurture the entrepreneurship capabilities of an individual and provide him with the necessary knowledge to start off on his own.

How should a candidate go about selecting the right course for himself?

A candidate should select the course based on his aptitude and interest. Some people prefer working with tools, some prefer interacting with other people, some are good at clerical jobs, some are good at field work, etc. A candidate can approach a career counselling centre for the right guidance in deciding the career for himself. Aspiring minds an NSDC partner and some SSCs have developed online aptitude tests.

What is recognition of prior learning (RPL)?

Recognition of Prior Learning (RPL) describes a process to evaluate learning acquired outside a structured education framework for the purpose of assigning due credits or certifications. In many cases, vocational education in India is passed on across generations and workers work in a certain trade without undergoing any formal education. The Directorate General of Employment & Training, MoLE allows private candidates having relevant experience in a trade to appear for the All India Trade Test on completion of which the candidate can acquire the National Trade Certificate. National Trade Certificate is a recognized qualification for recruitment to relevant posts and services in the Central/State Government establishments. Sector Skill Councils have also developed RPL programmes. NSDC partners like Labournet are conducting RPL in the construction and other sectors.

How can we leverage technology for better skill development?

Technology can help improve the quality of vocational skilling as well as reduce the costs. Digital video based content can help standardize the training across the country and remove the variability of quality of faculty. Simulator based skilling can help reduce the cost of equipment and consumables. Examples of this are driving, welding, etc. Distance education using web conferencing/video conferencing technologies can help bring a good teacher to a large distributed audience at the same time.

How can a digital system be leveraged for collaboration amongst multiple stakeholders in the skill ecosystem?

A common digital platform is the need of the hour to enable the various stakeholders in skilling i.e. government, industry bodies, job seekers/students, training institutions, certification bodies, NGOs, etc. to collaborate with each other. The platform will also reflect accurate and near real-time data on the skill demand, skill supply, gap therein, skilling capacity, placement ratio, wage scale, etc. This data will enable judicious policy formulation and planning for skill development.

How will Aadhar help in the skill development initiative?

Aadhar provides a method for uniquely identifying an individual. Aadhar enabled payment through linkages with banks and financial institutions provide a direct money transfer mechanism to the individual eliminating process overheads and inefficiencies. Aadhar will hence form the backbone of all skill development schemes targeted towards the individual and ensure the right targeting of efforts.

❑❑❑

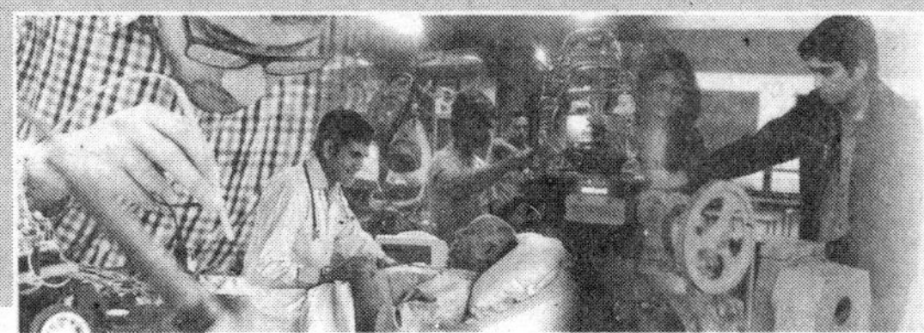

Bibliography

- CARNEGIE MELLON (2014) Assess Teaching and Learning. [Online] Available from https://www.cmu.edu/teaching/assessment/index.html
- DELOITTE (2013) Perspectives on Skill Development in Maharashtra: Matching Aspirations to Opportunities. New Delhi: Deloitte India
- DIRECTORATE GENERAL OF EMPLOYMENT & TRAINING (DGET) [2012] Trade Apprenticeship Training in India [Online] Available from http://dget.nic.in/publications/appren/ATS2011.pdf
- ERNSBERGER, L. (2012) Implementing National Qualification Framework(s) in India: Challenges of policy planning in context of human development, the demographic dividend and the informal sector. London: Institute of Education.
- ERNST & YOUNG (undated) Skills Gap Assessment for the State of Odisha: A district wise analysis. [Online] Available from http://nsdcindia.org/pdf/odisha-skill-gap-report.pdf
- FICCI (2006) The State of Industrial Training Institutes in India [Online] Available from http://www.b-able.in/Knowledge%20Bank/FICCI_The%20State%20of%20Industrial%20Training%20Institutes.pdf
- GREAT BRITAIN, UKIERI (2012) Credit Where Credit's Due: Experiences with the Recognition of Prior Learning and

Insights for India [Online] Available from http://www.ukieri.org/images/pdf/RPL_Report.pdf

- HARLEN, W. & R. DEAKIN CRICK (2002). A Systematic Review of the Impact of Summative Assessment and Tests on Students' Motivation for Learning. London: EPPI-Centre, Institute of Education.
- HEALTH AND SAFETY EXECUTIVE (HSE) [unknown] Human factors: Training & Competence [Online] Available from http://www.hse.gov.uk/humanfactors/topics/competence.htm
- ILO (2013a) Curriculum, Assessment & Certification under the Aajeevika Skills Development Programme (ASDP). New Delhi: ILO
- ILO (2013b) Skills Development Initiative: Modular Employable Skills Scheme. Feedback from the Field. New Delhi: ILO
- ILO (2014) National Consultative Forum in India on a Proposal for National Occupational Standards for Technical and Vocational Teachers/Trainers and Assessors. New Delhi: ILO
- Pravin Gupta. Business Innovation In The 21st Century, S. Chand & Company Ltd, New Delhi, 2009.
- Vasant Desai. Small Scale Enterprises and Entrepreneurship Eco-System, Himalaya Publishing House, Mumbai, 2011.
- National Skill Development policy, Government of India, labour.nic.in, 2014.
- Supriya Banerji. India Skill Report Confederation of Indian Industries, New Delhi, 2014.
- Dr. P. Kumar. Knowledge Paper on Skill Development in India-Learner First, FICCI, New Delhi, 2012.
- JOHNSON, J. (2006) Engaging India: Demographic dividend or disaster? [Online] The Financial Times Available from http://www.ft.com/cms/s/0/cd516aa8-749a-11db-bc76-0000779e2340.html#axzz368JD5yCR
- MINISTRY OF FINANCE (2013) NSQF Notification [Online] Available from http://www.skilldevelopment.gov.in/sites/default/files/resources/NQSF_Notification_English.pdf
- MINISTRY OF HOUSING & URBAN POVERTY ALLEVIATION (MHUPA) [2013] National Urban Livelihoods

Mission [Online] Available from http://mhupa.gov.in/NULM_Mission/docs/NULM_mission_document.pdf

- MINISTRY OF HUMAN RESOURCE DEVELOPMENT (MHRD) [2012] National Vocational Education Qualifications Framework (NVEQF): An Indian Perspective [Online] Available from http://www.asem-education-secretariat.org/imperia/md/content/asem2/events/2012_tvet_berlin/ws1_chauhan.pdf
- MINISTRY OF HUMAN RESOURCE DEVELOPMENT (MHRD) [2013a] Aajeevika Skill Development Programme Guidelines-2013 [Online] Available from http://www.nrlmskills.in/NewsEvents/Draft%20ASDP%20Guidelines2013-07-15/asdp%20guidelines%20as%20on%20110713.pdf
- MINISTRY OF HUMAN RESOURCE DEVELOPMENT (MHRD) [2013b] Aajeevika Skill.
- Development Programme Guidelines (Revised). New Delhi: Government of India.
- MINISTRY OF LABOUR AND EMPLOYMENT (MoLE) [2009] National Skill Development Policy [Online] Available from http://labour.nic.in/upload/uploadfiles/files/Policies/NationalSkillDevelopmentPolicyMar09.pdf
- MINISTRY OF LABOUR AND EMPLOYMENT (MoLE) [2014] Skill Development Initiative Scheme (SDIS): Based on Modular Employable Skills New Delhi: Government of India.
- MANIPAL CITY & GUILDS (2011) A Global Study to get India World-Ready. New Delhi: Manipal City & Guilds.
- MEHROTRA, S. et al (2013) Vocational Education and Training Reform in India: Business Needs and Lessons to be learned from Germany [Online] Available from http://www.bertelsmann-stiftung.de/bst/de/media/xcms_bst_dms_39337_39338_2.pdf
- Ministry of Finance (2013). Extraordinary Notification, Part 1, Section 2: National Skill Qualification Framework. New Delhi: Government of India.
- National Accreditation Board for Certification Bodies (NABCB) [2014]. Accreditation Schemes.

- Available from: http://www.qcin.org/nabcb/index.php
- National Accreditation Board for Education and Training (NABET) [2014] NABET: Introduction
- [Online] Available from http://nabet.qci.org.in/introduction_NABET.asp
- National Skill Development Corporation (NSDC) [2013a] National Occupational Standards (NOS) for SSCs [Online] Available from http://www.nsdcindia.org/pdf/nos-process-development.pdf
- National Skill Development Corporation (NSDC) [2013b] An Approach Paper for Setting up a Sector Skill Council [Online] Available from http://nsdcindia.org/pdf/approach-paper-ssc.pdf
- National Skill Development Corporation (NSDC) [2013c] FAQ QRC [Online] Available from http://nsdcindia.org/pdf/qrc-faq-nos-nos.pdf
- National Skill Development Corporation (NSDC) [2013d] Scheme Document of National Skill Certification and Monetary Award. New Delhi: NSDC
- National Skill Development Corporation (NSDC) [2013e] District wise skills gap study for the State of Haryana. [Online] Available from http://www.nsdcindia.org/pdf/haryana-sg-report.pdf
- National Skill Development Corporation (NSDC) [2013f] Executive Summary for the State of Maharashtra. [Online] Available from http://nsdcindia.org/pdf/maha-executive-summary.pdf [Accessed 10 May 2014]
- National Skill Development Corporation (NSDC) [2013g] Need Assessment Report on Building Trainers Skills in Vocational Employability. [Online] Available from http://nsdcindia.org/pdf/building-trainers-skills.pdf
- National Skill Development Corporation (NSDC) [2014] Process Manual: National Skill Certification and Monetary Reward Scheme v1.2. New Delhi: National Skill Development Corporation
- NATIONAL SKILL DEVELOPMENT AGENCY (NSDA) [2014] Skill Development Landscape in India [Online]

Available from http://www.skilldevelopment.gov.in/skill-landscape-in-india

- NEW INDIAN EXPRESS (2014) State Govt. to Implement NSQF The New Indian Express [Online] Available from http://www.newindianexpress.com/states/odisha/State-Govt-to-Implement-NSQF/2014/03/07/article2095387.ece
- ODISHA DIRECTORATE OF VOCATIONAL TRAINING (Odisha DVE) [2014] Action Plan on Vocational Education. Bhubaneswar: Government of Odisha.
- PANDE, S. (2014) Skill assessment agencies flourish, online tests preferred Business Today [Online] Available from http://businesstoday.intoday.in/story/skill-assessment-agencies-growth-in-India/1/202519.html
- PLANNING COMMISSION (2008a) Eleventh Five Year Plan (2007-2012): Social Sector, Vol. II [Online] Available from http://planningcommission.nic.in/plans/planrel/fiveyr/11th/11_v2/11th_vol2.pdf
- PLANNING COMMISSION (2008b) Eleventh Five Year Plan (2007-2012): Social Sector, Vol. III [Online] Available from http://planningcommission.nic.in/plans/planrel/fiveyr/11th/11_v2/11th_vol2.pdf
- RUKMINI, S. (2013) Demographic dividend at its peak. The Hindu [Online] Available from http://www.thehindu.com/news/national/demographic-dividend-at-its-peak/article5102093.ece
- RUST, C. (2002) Purposes and Principles of Assessment [Online] Available from http://www.brookes.ac.uk/services/ocsld/resources/briefing_papers/p_p_assessment.pdf
- SRINIVASAN, S. (2013) Skill Development Initiatives in India. Singapore: Institute of South Asian Studies
- UNESCO (2013) Global Inventory of NQFs: India [Online] Available from http://uil.unesco.org/fileadmin/keydocuments/LifelongLearning/en/UIL_Global_Inventory_of_NQFs_India.pdf
- WADHWANI FOUNDATION (2014) Hon'ble Chief Minister of Haryana, Shri Bhupinder Singh Hoods felicitates Wadhwani Foundation for successful implementation of Nation's first

pilot project under NVEQF. [Online] Available from http://wadhwani-foundation.org/wp-content/uploads/2014/02/Wadhwani-Foundation-felicitated-by-Honorable-Chief-Minister-of-Haryana-for-contribution-towards-quality-education-NVEQF.pdf

- WORLD BANK, (2011), 'Report No. 47 South Asia Human Development Sector–Affiliated Colleges in South Asia: Is Quality Expansion Possible?' [Online] Available from http://www-wds.worldbank.org/external/default/WDSContentServer/WDSP/IB/2011/12/14/000333037_201112 14235531/Rendered/PDF/660240WP00PUBL0iated0Colleges0Study.pdf
- http://www.nsdcindia.org
- http://www.skilldevelopment.gov.in
- http://nsdcudaan.com
- http://www.nsdcindia.org/pdf/worldskills.pdf http://dget.gov.in
- http://minorityaffairs.gov.in
- http://mhrd.gov.in
- http://wcd.nic.in
- http://www.nmew.gov.in
- http://www.mdoner.gov.in